A Passion for Victory

A Passion for Victory

Living Triumphantly Every Day

DR. BOB MOOREHEAD

HOWARD
PUBLISHING CO.
West Monroe, Louisiana

Our purpose at Howard Publishing is:

- *Instructing* believers toward a deeper faith in Jesus Christ
- *Inspiring* holiness in the lives of believers
- *Instilling* hope in the hearts of struggling people everywhere

Because he's coming again

A Passion for Victory

Published by Howard Publishing Co., Inc.
3117 North 7th Street, West Monroe, LA 71291-2227

Printed in the United States of America

Cover Design by LinDee Loveland
Edited by Philis Boultinghouse

Library of Congress Cataloging-in-Publication Data

Moorehead, Bob.
    A passion for victory : living triumphantly every day / Bob Moorehead.
       p. cm.
    ISBN 1-878990-64-0 (alk. paper)
    1. Christian life. I. Title.
BV4501.2.M5834 1996
248.4—dc20   96-23256
                                    CIP

IN DEDICATION

I dedicate this book to my son, Pastor Jeff Moorehead,
who himself has a passion for victory,
who has kept his life above reproach,
and who selflessly serves his Lord in full-time ministry.

■

CONTENTS

INTRODUCTION

I saw a man I hadn't seen for at least ten years. "How's your walk with the Lord doing?" I asked. His response was interesting. "Oh, I'm just hobbling along the best I can—some days ahead, some days behind—but I guess that's all you can expect."

Somewhere along the way, my friend had lost his passion for victory. It's hard to sustain a passion for something you believe is unattainable. Sadly, this depressing testimony is all too common among Christian people today. Only a minority of believers walk in consistent victory one year, five years, or ten years after their conversion to Christ.

Lester sat next to me on a bus of men going to a men's convention. Knowing we had a three-hour drive, I asked him, "How's it going?" His response was quite telling: "Well, Pastor, I'm scoring zero at my job, zero in my marriage, zero in my Christian walk, and zero with my friends." Lester was about twenty-eight or twenty-nine years old and three years into his marriage. Tall, blonde, muscular, and outgoing, you would never guess by looking at him that he was bombing out in his walk with the Lord—Lester had lost his passion for victory. So for almost three hours, I shared the basics of this book with him.

Throughout my years in ministry, I've come across countless Christians who struggle in their fellowship with Christ. They live like the first man I mentioned— "some days ahead, some days behind."

Perhaps that description even fits you. But by following the principles set forth in this book, you can renew your passion for victory; you can begin anew—and it's really not all that difficult! You *can* live triumphantly every day!

Remember, you have been saved to soar, not sink. You have been converted to conquer, not capitulate. You have been won to win!

The pages of this book reflect some basic principles I know to be true:

1. God wants you to get in and stay in victory.
2. Satan wants you to live in defeat.
3. As a Christian, you can *choose* whether to walk in victory or defeat.
4. It's easier to drift into defeat than to fight your way into victory and stay there.

5. Living and walking in victory isn't automatic; you have to passionately seize the victory.
6. All the components for consistent victory are available to you if you'll avail yourself of them.
7. Living in defeat day after day curtails your witness and damages your testimony.
8. Living in victory empowers your witness and affects people positively for Christ.
9. Victorious living is not complicated or impossible to attain.
10. Certain God-given principles must be adhered to if you are to walk in victory on a consistent basis.

I remember challenging Lester with the formula in this book. He wrote down the principles and began observing them one by one. He renewed his passion for victory, and today, he is a victorious, excited, on-fire Christian, with a consistency to his walk that he only dreamed of just a few months ago. The same can be true for you.

In the book of Acts, Christianity is referred to as "the Way" (Acts 24:14, 22). That means it's not just a body of cold, mechanical doctrines or statements—it's a way of life that's different from the non-Christian's. The over-arching characteristic of the Christian life is that it's victorious and triumphant. It's not a drag; it's not a downer; it's not a hardship. It's a way of life that enables us to emerge victorious and on top.

Living victoriously doesn't mean that we won't get sick, go broke, or experience severe hardship. It doesn't mean that everything will always go the way we think it ought to go. Nor does it mean we'll always have dry eyes and smiles on our faces. It *does* mean, though, that in the midst of the challenges of life, we will be soldiers who know and walk in the aura of victory. We may lose a few battles, but we will always win the war, because we are more than conquerors through him who loves us. Living victoriously means that we will walk tall, unafraid, unashamed, and undaunted by hardship—not in unrealistic denial, but in the truth that we're always victorious in Jesus Christ—even if we're bleeding!

This book is a practical guide to help every Christian *stay* on the victory road. It's not deeply theological, cognitive, or theoretical. It's a practical guide that will assist you in the task of actually experiencing victory.

Many years ago, I attended a black, holiness church in the deep south. I've forgotten the name of the church, the preacher's name, and the topic of the sermon, but I remember the preacher's closing words:

> When I walk, I walk in victory; when I sit, I sit in victory; when I drive, I drive in victory; when I sleep, I sleep in victory; when I talk, I talk in victory; when I eat, I eat in victory; when I work, I work in victory; when I pray, I pray in victory; when I preach, I preach in victory. As long as I live, I'll live in victory; and when I die, I'll die in victory. My middle name is victory, 'cause I serve a victorious God!

I call that a passion for victory! If you've been living on Defeat Avenue, welcome to Victory Boulevard.

Knowing Who You Are

- We are children of God
- We are heirs of God
- We are seated with Christ in the heavenly realms
- We are justified in the sight of God
- We are new creations
- We are righteous
- We are free from condemnation
- We have everything we need for life and godliness
- We are more than conquerors
- We are Spirit-indwelt
- We are ambassadors for Christ

The Identity Issue

Knowing Who You Are

E d is your typical thirty-one-year-old guy. Married with two small children, he earns his living as a forklift operator at the airport. He attends church with a fair amount of frequency, but confided in me one day that he felt like he was "sinking" in his Christian walk. He shared with me how he had been "sucked into" watching porn videos at lunch with two other guys. The videos got more and more explicit until he was watching X-rated porn of the worst kind almost daily. He found himself making sexual demands of his wife that were both per-verted and obnoxious. When she refused, he would become very angry and accuse her of running him into the arms of another woman. "I don't like what I've become," he confessed. My response to him was that, for starters, he needed to know who he was in Christ before he would ever have victory.

While understanding and accepting your true identity in Christ isn't the only way you claim victory, it's the first step; and you cannot circumvent it. Confusion about your identity makes you a sitting duck for Satan. One of the reasons many Christians don't live in victory is that they truly have an identity crisis. While we're not what we're going to be someday, we certainly aren't what we were! Let's look at who we are in Christ.

We Are Children of God

The Bible tells us that we were born not of "perishable seed" but of "imperishable" (1 Peter 1:23). If you're a Christian, you have royal blood flowing through your spiritual veins—you are a child of God!

> You are all sons of God through faith in Christ Jesus.
>
> Galatians 3:26

John the apostle encourages us with this bold affirmation:

> How great is the love the Father has lavished on us, that we should be called children of God! And that is what we are!
>
> 1 John 3:1

However, not everyone is a child of God—only those ᴏ, as Jesus said, have been "born again" (John 3:3). But ᵉ of us who are children of God have been born into a royal family. That means we count, we matter, and we have rights and privileges that nonbelievers don't have.

We Are Heirs of God

Before we gave our lives to Christ, we were slaves of sin. We have gone from being slaves to being heirs.

> You are no longer a slave, but a son; and since you are a son, God has made you also an heir.
> Galatians 4:7

Being an heir means that we're going to inherit something of value. Paul tells us the amazing extent of our inheritance:

> Now if we are children, then we are heirs—heirs of God and *co-heirs with Christ.*
> Romans 8:17

Co-heirs with Christ! That means that we inherit whatever Christ inherits, including, of course, eternal life. We're told in 1 Peter 1:3–6 that our inheritance is imperishable and unfading and that it cannot be spoiled.

Being an heir also means that we are deemed valuable by the one leaving the inheritance. The very fact that we're heirs of God and fellow heirs with Christ confirms the value God has placed on us. We count; we matter; we're important to God. He confirmed that fact by allowing his only Son to die for us on the cross.

We have an inheritance that the nonbeliever has no part of. It's easier to live victoriously when we know that we'll someday inherit it all.

We Are Seated with Christ in the Heavenly Realms

Oh, I know that *physically,* we're seated here (at a desk, in a chair, at home, on a plane), but *positionally,* we're seated with Christ.

> And God raised us up with Christ and seated us with him in the heavenly realms in Christ Jesus.
> Ephesians 2:6

What exactly does that mean? I believe Paul is seeing the future, but calling it a present reality. Someday, when our bodies cease to function, like a cocoon, we'll leave them for the "heavenly realms," for eternal houses "in heaven, not built by human hands" (2 Corinthians 5:1). There we'll be seated with Christ. To be "seated" with Christ is to be positioned in a place of honor. It's like when the host at a high-level function seats us at the head table right next to the guest of honor. Christ is the supreme honored one, and when we become Christians, God seats us right next to him. We've come from the "gutter-most" to the "utter-most." No wonder we sing about higher ground. We've been lifted to a new plane, with a new name, and a lost shame!

It's much easier to live triumphantly when we know we are victors by virtue of our exalted position.

We Are Justified in the Sight of God

The word *justification* means to be made just or righteous. Paul wrote,

Therefore, since we have been justified through faith, we have peace with God through our Lord Jesus Christ.

Romans 5:1

God not only *declares* us just, he *makes* us just. He does this through the work of Christ on the Cross, where Christ became the perfect sacrifice for our sin. Knowing that, because of our "position" in Christ, we are made just at our conversion and that we are kept just throughout our Christian walk gives us great incentive to walk in victory every day. Being justified means that our guilt has been replaced with exoneration—we've been acquitted! Thus, we can walk with heads erect and spirits high, because legally, in the eyes of God, we don't have to serve our sentence!

We Are New Creations

Paul said it plainly and with power,

Therefore, if anyone is in Christ, he is a new creation; the old has gone, the new has come!

2 Corinthians 5:17

As new creations, God has restored us to the innocence of the Garden of Eden. When God first created humans, he created them in innocence. They chose to sin, thus staining the whole human race. But God has miraculously restored us to that pristine purity, and we have become what we were intended to become when God made us.

As new creations, the guilt of our sin is gone—along with its accompanying condemnation—and God's express image is restored in us. We have become new and specially designed by a sovereign God. That design has put us on a new track where we are being "transformed into his likeness with every-increasing glory" (2 Corinthians 3:18). We are not what we once were. We now have the power to be victorious in our relationships, our speech, and any other challenge that may confront us.

We Are Righteous

Sound presumptuous? It certainly would be if I were talking about a righteousness I myself effected. But the Bible teaches that when I became a Christian, a metamorphosis took place that transformed me from being vile and filthy, thus condemned, to being totally righteous. In fact, the Bible actually says that I have become the "righteousness of God."

> God made him who had no sin to be sin for us, so that in him we might become the *righteousness* of God.
>
> 2 Corinthians 5:21

Positionally, "in him," I am now righteous—100 percent! I'm the first to admit that in *practice*, I fall short in my daily living, but because of my *position* before God, I have been made righteous by the transference of his righteousness onto me. This is called "imputed" righteousness. We neither created nor earned this righteousness, but we received it as part of our "acceptance package" from the beloved. In fact, if you want to know the degree to which you are righteous in the sight of God, John the apostle tells us.

> He who does what is right is righteous, just as he is righteous.
>
> 1 John 3:7

In other words, positionally, I am as righteous as Jesus Christ. No, I'm not there in my daily practice, but the goal of my life as a Christian is for my daily practice to line up with my position, and that is a never-ending process.

Being confident of my righteous identity in Christ makes it a lot easier to walk in consistent victory. I don't have to waste my energy and time hoping God will accept me when I trip up, because I know that he has imparted to me a perfect righteousness that will see me all the way through to heaven.

We Are Free from Condemnation

The Bible tells us that prior to accepting Christ, not only were we dead in our trespasses and sins, but we were under a curse (Galatians 3:10). That curse (condemnation) was removed the moment the blood of Christ cleansed me from all sin. The moment I was placed "in Christ" was the same moment I was placed "out of condemnation."

> Therefore, there is now no condemnation for those who are in Christ Jesus, because through Christ Jesus the law of the Spirit of life set me free from the law of sin and death.
>
> Romans 8:1–2

In the frontier days, a certain bank robber and killer was caught, tried, and sentenced to hang. One week before the execution was to take place, his older brother showed up at the sheriff's office with an unusual request. Since his brother was so young, he asked if he could hang in his place. Though at first resistant, the sheriff finally granted the request. The older brother died on the gallows in the place of his brother. That young man's condemnation was removed, and he was set free. This is exactly what Christ did for us. He stepped in, took our place, and died on the cross. His death freed us from the curse and condemnation that hung over us.

It's easier to walk in triumph every day when we know that the condemnation is gone and that we're free to live in victory.

We Have Everything We Need for Life and Godliness

His divine power has given us everything we need for life and godliness through our knowledge of him who called us by his own glory and goodness.

2 Peter 1:3

When we made Christ our Lord, God did a complete work in our lives, leaving no stone unturned—he gave us everything we need! His power not only blew apart our past and created our newness, it continues to sustain us and keep us from falling.

When we do slip, it's because we temporarily don't draw from what we have in Christ. How assuring to know that all the resources we need to be victorious have been given to us—all we have to do is draw from them.

We Are More Than Conquerors

> In all these things we are more than conquerors through him who loved us.
>
> Romans 8:37

Notice: we're not just conquerors, we're *more* than conquerors. What does that mean? It means we're not just victorious, we're super-victorious. Not that we ourselves won or effected our salvation but that God has placed us in the position of victor and has made us triumphant because of Christ.

We Are Spirit-Indwelt

Deity has opted to take up residence inside us! I know, it boggles my mind, too, but it's true.

> Don't you know that you yourselves are God's temple and that God's Spirit lives in you?
>
> 1 Corinthians 3:16

We're also told that we've received the *gift* of the Holy Spirit (Acts 2:38), that we've been *sealed* with the Holy Spirit (Ephesians 1:13), and that the Holy Spirit is a *permanent* resident in our lives (John 14:16). Amazing!

The Holy Spirit empowers us, guides us, leads us into all truth, produces fruit in us, and gifts us. Just realizing this makes it a lot easier to live the victorious life every day.

We Are Ambassadors for Christ

An ambassador is someone who lives in one country but represents another. That's us! We live in this world, but we represent our real home—heaven!

Paul put it like this in his second epistle to the Corinthians:

> We are therefore Christ's ambassadors, as though God were making his appeal through us. We implore you on Christ's behalf: Be reconciled to God.
>
> 2 Corinthians 5:20

Our identity in Christ is wrapped up in our purpose. As ambassadors, we represent Jesus Christ, and the theme of our ambassadorship is reconciliation to God. We're his personal representatives, left here to communicate the good news of the Gospel to people who haven't found what we've found—namely, life in Christ.

Not all of us can be a Dwight L. Moody or a Billy Graham. Not all of us can share the Gospel facts with eloquence. That's not important. What is important is that we represent the King as his personal ambassador in a way that honors him. As ambassadors, we don't talk about ourselves, we talk about the Lord and what he has done in our lives.

Just before he ascended to heaven, Jesus gave a final charge to the church. He said, "You will be my witnesses"

(Acts 1:8). A witness is someone who testifies about what he has seen and heard. As witnesses of Christ, we're obligated to tell others what we've experienced in Christ. The reason Christ didn't take us to heaven the moment we became Christians is that he intends for us to seriously affect other people's lives for him. The most convincing argument is a satisfied customer. If Christ has made a significant difference in our lives, we need to tell others about it.

Of course, this sometimes demands that we build relationships so we can earn the right to talk about eternal things. This takes time and deliberate effort, but as ambassadors of Christ, this is our mission.

M any Christians are defeated by Satan because they forget who they are and what they're worth to God. I read the following description of our worth many years ago and have never forgotten it.

> A man weighing 176 pounds lives in a body that contains enough fat to make nine bars of soap, enough iron to make one nail, enough lime to whitewash one chicken coop, enough phosphorous to make a few hundred match heads, enough water to fill a nine-gallon can, and enough sulfur to de-flea one small dog. In all, he is worth about $23.79 on the open market.

Well, I'm glad we're worth more than that to God! When we remember who we are in Christ, we have a greater chance of living in daily triumph.

Remember Ed? Of course you do. Ed experienced defeat mainly because he forgot who he was in Christ. He forgot that he was forgiven, cleansed, and the recipient of God's grace. He forgot that the Holy Spirit lived within him. But after spending a few weeks with a men's encouragement team going over these eleven identities that are ours in Christ, he regained his passion for victory and stands firm today.

Remember—when we clearly understand *who* we are in Christ, we'll be eager to *do* what we can for Christ.

Prayer

O God, remind me of who I am in Christ. Help me remember that I'm forgiven, righteous, whole, filled with your Spirit, justified, and your personal representative. Help me in my daily walk to be who I am and to delight in my identity. Help me to bask in my new name, my new destination, my new companion, and my new agenda.

Amen.

Knowing What You Have

- Forgiveness of sins
- The Holy Spirit
- His promises
  Power
  Victory through faith
  Eternal security
  Confidence
  Heaven
  Complete access
  Hope
  Eternal life

Reveling in Your Resources

Knowing What You Have

I n almost forty years of ministry, I've discovered that one of the biggest reasons many people live their whole Christian lives in utter defeat—with no passion for victory—is ignorance! That's right. I don't know any other way to say it. Ignorance! They simply don't know (or have forgotten) what they have in Christ.

When you became a Christian, you came into resources that had not been available to you before. They are both rich and plentiful; in fact, they are inexhaustible. Paul said it most clearly:

> All things are yours . . . and you are of Christ, and Christ is of God.
>
> 1 Corinthians 3:21, 23

Wow! When we received Christ, we got it *all*. I believe God wants us to revel in what is legally ours—certainly not in an arrogant or boastful way—but to have it all and utilize none of it is a travesty.

I once read about a man who booked a cruise from Europe to America in the early 1900s. It took him three years to save the money to buy his ticket. He finally scraped together just enough money for the ticket; but he had none to spare, so he packed a supply of cheese and crackers, all he could afford, to eat on the trip. Every day he rationed a scant supply out to himself. But toward the end of the journey, he realized that he had miscalculated the number of days the trip would take, and with four days to go, his dwindling supply was all but gone. For the next two days he ate only crumbs, and on the third day he simply drank water. The captain of the ship noticed that he was only drinking water and asked why. "I ran out of my supply of food," the man replied. "Supply of food? Didn't you know that three meals a day were included in the price of your ticket?"

Can you imagine? He had a wonderful banquet available three times a day, yet he was eating like a pauper. Sadly, that's how many Christians travel through life. While their position in Christ entitles them to countless blessings, they live as if their God supplies them nothing. Let's take a look at what we have in him.

Forgiveness of Sins

In him we have redemption through his blood, *the forgiveness of sins,* in accordance with the riches of God's grace that he lavished on us with all wisdom and understanding.

Ephesians 1:7–8

That means we live in daily forgiveness, as the blood of Jesus constantly cleanses us from all sin (1 John 1:7). Satan accuses us and reminds us that we fall short, that we've sinned, that we're not worthy. When he reminds you of your past, make sure you remind him of his future! His future is clear—he will be thrown into the lake of fire! (Revelation 20:10). Knowing that the accuser can't legally accuse us and make it stick helps us live in perpetual victory. We don't have to slip around, red faced and feeling inferior. The blood of Christ has forgiven our sins, and God sees us as if we had never sinned.

The Holy Spirit

The Holy Spirit indwells us. He is resident in us. We're told that when we were saved, he came to take up permanent residence in us.

Among his ministries as head resident of our lives, he

- guides us into all truth (John 16:12–13)

- empowers us (Ephesians 3:16; Acts 1:8)

- seals us (Ephesians 1:13; 2 Corinthians 1:20–22)

- intercedes for us (Romans 8:26)

- kills our carnal pursuits (Romans 8:13)

- leads us (Romans 8:14; Acts 16:6–9)

- confirms our sonship (Romans 8:15–16)

- provides adequate fruit in our lives (Galatians 5:22–26)
- gifts us with spiritual gifts (1 Corinthians 12:11)
- fills us (controls us) (Ephesians 5:18)
- becomes the instrument of God's love to us (Romans 5:5)

Just knowing that the third person of the Trinity has opted to make his permanent home inside me is enough reason for me to live and walk in total victory. As I struggle with this world system, I don't need to wonder if I'll win.

> The one who is in you is greater than the one who is in the world.
> 1 John 4:4

I have a leg up on the enemy because of who dwells inside me. He gives me ongoing victory! I'm not alone in my battles, temptations, struggles, and pressures. He's there inside me as God's personal guarantee so that I may be bold and positive about the Lord and my position in him.

His Promises

When I became a Christian (ancient history), it was customary in the church for people to stand up and speak out a promise of God. People would stand and say,

> "He'll never leave or forsake me."
>
> "He'll give me power for temptation."
>
> "He'll give me comfort."
>
> "He'll make a way where there is no way."

And on and on the testimonies would go. But the practice eventually ceased, and a whole generation of Christians grew up without hearing an emphasis on the promises of God. The fact is, most churches never even sing the old hymn "Standing on the Promises." Many are only "sitting on the premises."

There is a powerful section of Scripture in 2 Peter that sums all this up.

> His divine power has given us everything we need for life and godliness through our knowledge of him who called us by his own glory and goodness. Through these he has given us his *very great and precious promises,* so that through them you may participate in the divine nature and escape the corruption in the world caused by evil desires.
>
> 2 Peter 1:3–4

God's promises weren't given to us just to make us feel good or happy; they were given so that we might walk in total victory.

The following chorus, which I once taught kids in Vacation Bible School, can encourage us adults today:

> Every promise in the book is mine,
> Every chapter, every verse, every line.
> All are blessings of his love divine,
> Every promise in the book is mine.

This little song helped teach the children to believe and revel in his promises. Let's look at some of the precious and very great promises he has given us.

Power

Remember, it's "his divine power" that has granted to us all things. Paul said in Ephesians 1,

> His incomparably great power for us who believe . . . is like the working of his mighty strength, which he exerted in Christ when he raised him from the dead.
>
> Ephesians 1:19–20

In other words, the power within us is the same kind of power God used to raise Jesus from the dead. I don't know how many "kinds" of power God has, but if that were the only kind he has for believers, it would be enough! If it's powerful enough to raise Jesus from death, it will have no problem raising us to live victorious lives.

That power enables us to

- witness

- overcome temptation

- pray

- worship

- serve

- be bold in our testimony

- overcome addictions

- pull down strongholds

Paul prayed for the Ephesians:

> I pray that out of his glorious riches he may strengthen you with *power* through his Spirit in

your inner being, so that Christ may dwell in your hearts through faith. And I pray that you, being rooted and established in love, may have *power*, together with all the saints, to grasp how wide and long and high and deep is the love of Christ.

Ephesians 3:16–18

We, too, may be empowered to grasp the vastness of God's love. That's power!

Victory through Faith

In his little epistle, John wrote to those who were going through difficult times. He said,

This is the victory that has overcome the world, even our faith.

1 John 5:4

Faith is the victory that overcomes. God has promised to equip us with that faith and to supply enough of it so that we can win the battle. It's up to us to appropriate it. In other words, we have the victory; we just need to appropriate it.

Eternal Security

Many Christians succumb to defeat because they aren't secure in their position. Jesus said,

I give them eternal life, and they shall never perish; no one can snatch them out of my hand.

John 10:28

What a promise! Not only has Jesus promised to protect us from any who would try to snatch us from him, he's promised that he will never drive us away or cast us out—even when we disappoint him.

> All that the Father gives to me will come to me, and whoever comes to me I will never drive away.
>
> John 6:37

It's a lot easier for me to live in victory when I don't have to hassle with whether or not I'm going to lose my salvation.

Confidence

God has enabled us to live and walk in absolute confidence, not because of our prowess or sharpness, but because of his.

> Such confidence as this is ours through Christ before God. Not that we are competent in ourselves to claim anything for ourselves, but our competence comes from God. He has made us competent.
>
> 2 Corinthians 3:4–6

Lack of confidence is usually rooted in lack of competence. If we understand, from the start, that our competence comes from God, our confidence level will be what it's supposed to be.

Heaven

Jesus personally promised heaven to us.

If I go and prepare a place for you, I will come
back and take you to be with me that you also
may be where I am.

John 14:3

This is perhaps the most precious promise a believer
has. Jesus will personally come back to this earth and take
us to be with him. Earlier in John 14, Jesus said he was
going to prepare a place for us. That place is heaven. A
full description of heaven is given in Revelation 21. We
are promised that it will be a beautiful place, but heaven's
greatest attraction is that Jesus is there.

Complete Access

Recently I passed through Paris on my way from Tel
Aviv to New York. I had to produce my passport and
have it stamped. At the next booth, upon showing my
stamped page, I was waived on through to catch my
plane. Whew! What if I had not had a stamped passport?
I would have had no access.

Paul says,

Therefore, since we have been justified through
faith, we have peace with God through our Lord
Jesus Christ, through whom we have gained
access by faith into this grace in which we now
stand.

Romans 5:1–2

When you were saved, it took a heap of God's grace to
cover your sin. But have you ever stopped to think that
you still need grace to live and walk victoriously? God's
grace got you in, and his grace keeps you in. As a Christ-

ian, you have ongoing, limitless access to this grace so that it can continue to cover the sins you commit on a daily basis.

Not only do you have access to grace, you also have access, through prayer, to the very throne room of God. We're told to

> approach the throne of grace with confidence, so that we may receive mercy and find grace to help us in our time of need.
>
> Hebrews 4:16

The door between the Holy Place and the Holy of Holies is wide open now, no more to close. We now have access to God and all his resources.

Hope

People can live without possessions, even without good health, but they cannot survive long when void of hope. By definition, hope concerns things we cannot see. The Hebrews writer said this:

> We have this hope as an anchor for the soul, firm and secure.
>
> Hebrews 6:19

Paul said in Romans 5:5 that "hope does not disappoint us." By this definition, hope is not simply *wishing* for something we don't really think we'll get; hope is *expecting* God to deliver what he has promised. Hope might also be defined as an irrepressible optimism about the future, based on the promise of God that his glorious will, will be done.

Hope is the confidence that all our tomorrows are in the hands of God, that all wrongs will be righted, and that all injustice will disappear. Hope is believing that someday we'll get a new body, that someday Christ will gather his church out of this world, and that we will reign with him forever and ever.

First Timothy 6:17 tells us that the object of our hope is God himself. And where does our hope come from?

> Through the encouragement of the Scriptures we might have hope.
>
> Romans 15:4

That's exactly right! Our hope springs from not only the promises, but from the projections made in God's Word.

Eternal Life

The grave is not the end for believers. There's more. There's better. The Bible calls it *eternal life.* And this eternal life is not just something we'll have in the *future,* the Bible tells us we have eternal life *right now* as a present possession.

> Whoever believes in the Son has eternal life.
>
> John 3:36

This means that when we accept Jesus Christ as our Savior, we are given the gift of eternal life. Eternal life isn't just quantitative, it's qualitative. It's a quality of life found only in Jesus Christ, and its quality is such that we can take it into eternity. Oh, by the way, we don't have to guess about eternal life if we're saved:

I write these things to you who believe in the
name of the Son of God so that you may *know*
that you have eternal life.

1 John 5:13

We can know we have eternal life, even though we
haven't come into the fullness of all of it yet. God wants
us to live in the confidence that we will live forever with
him. When we have that kind of confidence, we will walk
the road of victory, not defeat—no matter how bad the
circumstances get.

So, what do we have in Christ? We have it all. We're
fellow heirs with Christ: all that's coming to him is
also coming to us.

Several years ago I read a sad story in the newspaper
about a crippled woman who was confined to a wheelchair. When her parents died, she was left to cope all
alone. No brothers, no sisters, no living relatives. She
lived in a small, cramped apartment. She earned money
to pay her rent and buy scant supplies of food by knitting,
even though it hurt her crippled hands and fingers terri-
bly. For forty-two years she barely squeaked by. One day,
an elderly man, a friend of her parents, knocked on her
door to say hello while he was in her city. When he saw
how she was living, he was appalled.

"Why are you living in such abject poverty?" he asked.

"Since my parents died, I've tried to support myself,
but it's been difficult."

"Don't you know about the fortune willed to you by your parents?"

In shock, she said, "What fortune?"

He went on to tell her of the hundreds of thousands of dollars her parents had left her in a trust account—enough to take care of her for the rest of her life. When the friend of the family began contacting the attorneys and the banks, he and they discovered that a terrible mistake had been made: she had never been notified of her great fortune. Over the past forty-two years, the trust had accumulated so much interest that its worth was now in the millions; but she had lived most of her life in poverty because she didn't know what was rightfully hers!

How many Christians live in defeat, spiritual poverty, and depression because they don't know the riches they have in Christ. *Know your assets!*

Prayer

Lord, you've provided everything I need to live this incredible Christian life you've given me. I rejoice in those resources. Grant me the wisdom to draw from that bottomless well of your power, your presence, your wisdom, and your inspiration. Enable me to bask in the limitless assets of my life in you.

Amen.

Putting the Earthly to Death

- ■ **Kill the culprits**
  Sexual immorality
  Impurity
  Lust
  Evil desires
  Greed
  Anger
  Rage
  Malice
  Slander
  Filthy language
  Lying

- ■ **Work the plan**
  Acknowledge your responsibility
  Assemble a list of your sins
  Be accountable to fellow Christians
  Aspire to things above
  Acquire what is good
  Assess yourself

THREE

Killing the Culprits

Putting the Earthly to Death

I'll call him Dale. Married for only a couple of years, this twenty-eight-year-old stock-market worker wrote me a lengthy letter. He became a Christian his senior year in high school and was very active in his faith, even through his college years. He fell in love with the president of a sorority at his university, and they married. The financial pressures of marriage brought reality into sharp focus. In order to meet his new responsibilities, he had to get up every day at 3:45 A.M. so he could be in his office by the time the stock market opened on the east coast. His work day began at five in the morning. He worked around beautiful women every day, and he soon found himself eaten up with sexual lust. All of this blended together to undermine his growth as a Christian. In fact, as his letter termed it, he was "sinking a little deeper every day." He even signed his letter, "Your sinking friend, Dale."

We met and talked. It was obvious that he was no longer walking in victory, so I asked him this question: "Have you been on a killing spree?"

With shock he responded, "I haven't sunk that low." But the killing spree I was talking about is not only biblically permissible, it's actually commanded. Living triumphantly demands that we kill the culprits that are out to defeat us. Hear what Scripture says:

> *Put to death,* therefore, whatever belongs to your earthly nature.
>
> Colossians 3:5

There are two obvious assumptions in that command.

1. You (not God) are to do it. It's your responsibility.

2. You have the power or ability to do it, or it would not have been commanded.

Kill the Culprits

The only time that it's perfectly legal for the believer to murder is when the victim is his or her "earthly nature." Paul says, "put it to death": kill it, destroy it, get rid of it, pulverize it, decimate it, burn it, drown it, vanquish it. In the Greek language, this command is in the aorist tense, which is punctiliar, meaning a once-for-all action. In other words, be decisive, deliberate, purposeful—not casual—

act with gusto and abandon. Treat it like a class-A emergency, and get the job done!

Then Paul gets very specific: he lists the culprits that we are to kill in our lives.

Sexual Immorality

The original Greek word behind this English translation means any kind of sex act perpetrated outside the bonds of marriage. Homosexual acts, bestiality, fornication, adultery, perverted acts, premarital sex, extramarital sex, and all kinds of deviant sexual behavior—they're all included in that one word. We're to kill these things in our lives.

Impurity

This is a general impurity of thought and deed. It deals mostly with impure thinking and fantasizing brought on by outside stimuli, such as pornography.

Lust

This word literally means a craving desire for something. It can be something sexual or nonsexual. It can be a craving for illicit sex, for material wealth, for position and status, or for recognition. Most of the places in the Bible where this word is used are connected with inordinate desire. We're talking about the kind of desire that controls us, that drives us, that compels us.

Evil Desires

We could easily translate this "forbidden desires." These desires are not of God, and if fulfilled will become an evil force in our lives. We ought always to ask, "Are my desires what God desires for my life? Are they clean, pure, wholesome, and in line with the revealed will of God?" If not, they're *evil* desires.

Greed

This word has to do with selfishness and with wanting something that isn't ours and never can be; but we want it all the same. I find it very interesting that it's listed right along with sexual sins. In fact, Paul calls it "idolatry," because the thing or person desired becomes a god that we end up worshiping above God. Greedy people are never satisfied with what they have; they always want more. Jesus hit greed and covetousness very hard in his teaching.

> Watch out! Be on your guard against all kinds of greed; a man's life does not consist in the abundance of his possessions.
>
> Luke 12:15

I suppose all of us are afflicted with this sin to one degree or another, but in Colossians 3 Paul makes an appeal for us to give it up, to lay it aside, and to get a right, biblical view of "things."

Anger

Paul begins a second list in verse 8. He tells the readers, "You must rid yourselves of all such things as these," and anger tops the list. While all anger isn't sin, it's implied here that this kind of anger is. Vine's *Expository Dictionary of New Testament Words* says that this anger is a "settled or abiding condition of mind, frequently with a view to taking revenge."

It's true that Jesus got angry with the money changers and with those buying and selling in the temple, but his anger was based on the fact that his Father had been offended. He was angry that God's house of prayer had been turned into a den of robbers, thus perverting the temple.

Our anger seldom arises from such noble origins. If our hearts are continually filled with anger, we will not reap the joy that forgiveness and goodwill bring into our lives.

Rage

This is a strong word. It means the kind of anger that sends us into an uncontrollable rage that goes on and on. It has to do with an unleashed wrath. Today, we call it "losing it."

Malice

This word means "desire to cause pain, injury, or distress to another." It implies "a deep-seated often unexplainable desire to see another suffer" (*Merriam Webster's Collegiate Dictionary*, 10th edition). Such an attitude has no place in the Christian's heart. Paul tells us to get rid of it.

Slander

Slander is speech that is injurious to another's good name or that destroys another's reputation. It means dragging someone's name through the mud via gossip or accusations. It's often referred to as "character assassination" because it can virtually kill one's reputation. *Libel* refers to written as well as spoken words that defame another's character. People are sued daily for libel. Neither slander nor libel have any place in the Christian life.

The old adage "Sticks and stones may break my bones, but words will never hurt me" just isn't so, and we know it. Words can cut deeper than a knife, and once spoken cannot be easily retrieved, if at all.

Filthy Language

Nothing is more disappointing than to hear a believer spew out filthy, lewd, or blasphemous language, as though such language helps get his point across. This not only dishonors God, it shatters any effectiveness one's testimony may have. The word in the Greek actually means abusive language. Its literal meaning is "obscene speech." The Revised Standard Version calls it "foul talk." The New American Standard Bible calls it "abusive speech." Whatever you call it, it needs to be ruthlessly dealt with. If we "are what we say," this kind of language will keep us from living victoriously.

Lying

In verse 9 Paul says, "Do not lie to each other." There are many forms of lying and many ways to get around the truth, but it's all lying. Paul said, "Get rid of it! Put it to death!"

What a list. What a task. But if we would live the victorious life, all of these things must go, and it is our responsibility to see that they are "murdered."

Work the Plan

By now, I can hear some of you saying, "Tell us how; tell us how! We know we're to murder those things that keep us from living victoriously, but how can we successfully pull this off?" I'm glad you asked. Below is a step-by-step plan to keep you on the victory way.

Acknowledge Your Responsibility

It is your responsibility to initiate the killing spree. Acknowledging this is half the battle. Many people just fold their hands and say, "Lord, I can't do this; you do it for me." Of course there is a sense in which God does it for you, in that it's his power and his sovereignty that are at work in your life, but you must initiate the action. You can't stay on Victory Boulevard by placing your life on "automatic pilot." Oh, no!

We are exhorted again and again in Scripture to do certain things. Look at some of the things we're commanded to do: we're to "stand fast," "present our bodies as living sacrifices," "love one another," "give thanks," "not put out the Spirit's fire," "hold on to the good," "avoid every kind of evil," "pray constantly," and "give." Yes, God keeps our salvation and position in Christ in place, but we are called on to "put to death" and "get rid of" all that is detrimental to living out that salvation on a daily basis.

Assemble a List of Your Sins

The list from Colossians 3 may just be the tip of your iceberg. Maybe you struggle with other things like overeating, jealousy, pride, materialism, gossip, etc. You can't kill the culprits in your life till you line them up! I made a list of sins one New Year's day, then put a check mark by the ones I was having trouble with. Try it.

    __ gossip

    __ anger

    __ malice

    __ sexual lust

    __ impatience

    __ swearing

    __ greed and avarice

    __ selfishness

    __ faultfinding

    __ gluttony

    __ lying (exaggerations)

The list could go on and on. Maybe you'll want to make your own. It may sound like an elementary exercise, but if you really want to live triumphantly every day, you'll take the time and pay the price!

Be Accountable to Fellow Christians

Don't even think of trying to kill the culprits without some accountability in your life. Oh, I know we're accountable to God, but we need brothers and sisters to whom we're accountable as well. Find some people who will not be intimidated by you and who will be willing to hold your feet to the fire. I have an accountability group of six men I dearly love. They pull no punches and aren't afraid to ask the hard questions. I submit to their hard questions because I know me all too well. I know those areas where I am prone to sin. They know them too. I am willing to be "nailed" when nailing needs to be done. I've asked these men to confront me when they see me getting cynical, overly tired, overscheduled, critical, unpleasant to be around, impatient with others, or sloppy in my preaching. And guess what? They do! Does it sting a bit? A lot! But I need it to keep me on track. Don't even think of trying to "put to death" anything in your life without the motivation and encouragement that accountability brings.

Aspire to Things Above

We're told repeatedly in Scripture to seek those things that are above—godly things, spiritual things, biblical things. I love what Paul urged us to do in Philippians:

> Finally, brothers, whatever is true, whatever is noble, whatever is right, whatever is pure, whatever is lovely, whatever is admirable—if anything is excellent or praiseworthy—think about such things.
>
> Philippians 4:8

To help you seek those things, start your day in the Word and in prayer. Jesus did, and if he felt the need to do it, who do we think we are that we could forfeit such a necessary beginning to our days?

Acquire What Is Good

Seize the good, the right, the true, the honorable, the pure. Paul put it this way:

> Hate what is evil; cling to what is good.
> Romans 12:9

Develop an appetite for the good and the holy. That begins with *knowing* that this is what God wants you to do. We live in a soiled world, a world that barrages us with its filth and lewdness. But the Bible says,

> Be holy, because I am holy.
> 1 Peter 1:16

Just as people "develop" a taste for certain foods, we need to develop a taste for holiness.

Assess Yourself

How are you doing? What is your progress?

Instead of assessing your IQ, how about measuring your KQ (Killing Quotient). Ask yourself, "Am I working the plan to kill those things that are trying to kill me? Am I taking hold of the authority God has given me to put to death those things he doesn't want in my life?" The Bible says,

> A man ought to examine himself.
> 1 Corinthians 11:28

Regularly evaluating and assessing my progress is vital; otherwise, I will have no clue as to how I'm doing. Assessment is a must. If I go on a diet, I must submit to a set of scales to see if I'm progressing. If I commit to having a quiet time daily, I need some measuring device to reflect my progress. Without evaluation, look for frustration!

O h, you may be wondering about Dale. Dale had not realized that God was holding him responsible for killing the culprits that were keeping him from living victoriously. But after he became aware of his responsibility, he made a list of the culprits found in Colossians 3. During his daily quiet time, he focused on just one culprit per week, sometimes taking two weeks to work on the ones that plagued him the most—like impurity and lust. With the help of a good accountability group of three other guys and the discipline of the Word, Dale dealt with those culprits once and for all. Is he still tempted from time to time? Absolutely. In weak moments does he find his mind gravitating toward those evil thoughts? To be sure. But in it all, he knows he's more than a conqueror through Christ (Romans 8:37). He no longer signs his notes to me as "Your sinking friend" but as "Your brother in victory!" Dale's passion for victory has been rekindled, and he is living victoriously today because he killed the culprits that sought to defeat him.

Surely you recall the story of Saul in the Old Testament. When God told Saul to completely destroy the Amalekites, Saul went in with plans to destroy them. But when it came time to actually *do* it, he did not destroy them completely. God was displeased. At the end of Saul's life, it was an Amalekite who slayed him. *That which God had told him to destroy stood in the end to destroy him!*

We'll either destroy those culprits or they'll destroy us! It's that simple. But don't expect to destroy them apart from the Word and prayer. While the responsibility is ours, we must draw on the resources that God provides.

Two springs ago I planted a very small vegetable garden. I planted onions, carrots, and tomatoes. I watered, fertilized, and checked daily to see what was happening. But I failed to do one thing. I failed to *weed* the garden. You know the rest of the story. The weeds grew at an alarming rate. They were healthy, green, vibrant, big, and consuming. The vegetables? What vegetables? They were driven out and consumed by the weeds. I failed to "kill the culprits," and I paid the price of a garden gone to seed. The same principle holds true in the spiritual realm. The Christian life is like a garden—and God won't do the weeding for you. It's up to you! Get that hoe and rake, and go to work—kill those culprits!

Prayer

Father, grant me the skilled hands of a surgeon as I excise from my life all the rubbish that doesn't belong there. I pray for daily direction as I do radical surgery from time to time, removing from my life the unwanted and unneeded debris that curbs my appetite for you, and tries to damage my testimony. Give me the courage, as you have given me the strength, to truly put to death what is earthly in me.

Amen.

Renewing Your Mind

- ## What mind renewal isn't
  Positive thinking
  Transcendental meditation
  Hypnosis
  New thinking habits

- ## What mind renewal is
  Thinking like Christ
  Thinking about God
  Controlling your "mind-set"
  Dwelling on God's Word
  Choosing positive companions

- ## Enemies of renewal
  A busy schedule
  A negative mood
  Bitterness
  Selfishness
  Worldliness
  Anger

FOUR

Laundering Your Life

Renewing Your Mind

I've heard it said that a perfectionist is someone who puts newspapers underneath his cuckoo clock at night! But I've noticed something about perfectionists—they're not perfect! Try as they may to cross every "t" and dot every "i," they never quite pull off perfection, and it drives them nuts!

While *perfection* is out of our reach, *renewal* isn't. As Christians, we can choose to renew our minds—to think in a whole new way. And if we have a passion for victory, we must choose to learn the secret of what it really means to renew our minds. Paul gave us believers this injunction:

> Do not conform any longer to the pattern of this
> world, but be transformed by the *renewing of your
> mind.*
>
> Romans 12:2

The word "transformed" comes from the Greek word *metamorphousthe,* from which we get our word *metamorphosis.* It means change from the inside out. The key to this change is the mind. In other words, our thinking has to radically change—so radically that we can't pull it off alone.

What Mind Renewal Isn't

Sometimes, before we can understand the meaning of a concept, we need to deal with common misconceptions and get them out of the way, so we can see the truth more clearly. So it is with *mind renewal.* Before we look at what it is, let's make sure we understand what it isn't.

Positive Thinking

Mind renewal isn't developing the power of positive thinking. I once picked up a little pamphlet in a hospital waiting room that said if we think positively, speak positively, and look positively, we can totally renew our way of thinking, and life will become positive. Such views are born out of the "positive confession" movement that says you can think and speak conditions into existence that don't now exist, if you will think and speak hard enough. Besides being unscriptural, that kind of thinking is not even practical, and those who pursue it are usually in for a great letdown.

Transcendental Meditation

Mind renewal is not transcendental meditation. Many would have you believe that if you can properly meditate in a lotus position, you can "connect" with the appropriate thought waves floating around in the universe and thereby foster calm, creativity, and spiritual well-being. Gurus of this thinking pass it off as renewal of the mind, touting it as a panacea for those whose negative thoughts imprison them in a dungeon of despair.

Hypnosis

Mind renewal is not achieved by hypnosis. Those who submit their minds to the control of others have, at best, a temporary surge of a pseudo-renewal in their thought processes; but soon, reality sets in, and they need another session.

New Thinking Habits

The renewing of the mind is not merely a change of thinking habits. Many people believe if they just "change the way they think," they can renew their minds and spirits and get back on a positive track.

What Mind Renewal Is

Now that we've seen what mind renewal isn't, we're ready to look at what it is. Paul talked much about our minds and their renewal.

Do not lie to each other, since you have taken off your old self with its practices and have put on

> the new self, which is being *renewed* in knowledge in the image of its Creator.
>
>   Colossians 3:9–10

Again, in writing the church at Ephesus, he reminded his brothers and sisters,

> You were taught, with regard to your former way of life, to put off your old self, which is being corrupted by its deceitful desires; [and] to be *made new in the attitude of your minds.*
>
>   Ephesians 4:22–23

What choices can you make in order to begin the process of mind renewal? Let's start with the following biblical principles.

Thinking like Christ

Mind renewal means choosing to develop the kind of thinking that Christ had. In Philippians, Paul said,

> Your attitude should be the same as that of Christ Jesus.
>
>   Philippians 2:5

The Revised Standard Version says,

> Have this *mind* among yourselves which is yours in Christ Jesus.

In other words, *think like Christ.* Of course, no one knows completely how Christ thought; what we do know, we learn through his words and deeds. He taught forgiveness, love, humility, patience, acceptance, servanthood, dependence, and many more godly traits. There is only one way to think like Christ: study his life, his demeanor, his spirit, his words, and his deeds. The only way to do that is to get into God's Word often and thoroughly.

Thinking about God

Renewing the mind is *keeping* the mind on God. Thinking about God continually isn't natural for us, but we can learn to do it by practicing the presence of God. In Psalm 89, the psalmist says,

> Blessed are those who have learned to acclaim you, who walk in the light of your presence, O Lord.
>
> Psalm 89:15

By learning to walk in the presence of the Lord, we can train our minds to steadfastly trust in him:

> You will keep in perfect peace him whose mind is steadfast, because he trusts in you.
>
> Isaiah 26:3

Our goal here is to have a "steadfast" mind. We *can* develop the habit of thinking about the greatness of God—it can be done by a conscious act of the will.

Controlling Your "Mind-Set"

Renewal of the mind has to do with choosing to control what our minds are "set" on. As Christians, we can set our minds on material things, base things, fleshly things, and carnal things, or we can set them on godly things. Romans says it clearly:

> Those who live according to the sinful nature
> have their *minds set* on what that nature desires;
> but those who live in accordance with the Spirit
> have their *minds set* on what the Spirit desires.
>   Romans 8:5

Those are powerful words because they put the responsibility squarely on our shoulders. In what direction is your mind set to think? Where do you *aim* your mind? Paul said in Colossians 3:2 that we're to set our "minds on things above, not on earthly things." We control the setting of our minds; we can set our minds on anything we desire. But as believers, we're commanded to set them on things above, on spiritual things. This is hard because we live in a material world—but it can be done. How? Only by funneling every thought we have through the sieve of Scripture. Again, the Word of God and renewal of the mind are inseparable.

Dwelling on God's Word

> Let the word of Christ dwell in you richly as you
> teach and admonish one another.
>   Colossians 3:16

Not only are we to let God's Word dwell in us, we are to let it dwell in us richly. I'm not talking simply about a lot of Bible reading. I'm talking about letting Scripture be absorbed into your mind and heart so that when Satan comes to take you under, you can ward him off the same way Jesus did.

When Jesus was tempted sorely by the devil, he said, "It is written. . . ." He fought power with power: his power was the authority of God's Word. Satan melts when a volley of Scripture is quoted.

The Psalms attest to the extraordinary value and power of God's Word:

> But his delight is in the law of the Lord, and on his law he meditates day and night.
>
> Psalm 1:2

Again,

> I have hidden your word in my heart that I might not sin against you.
>
> Psalm 119:11

The psalmists teach us to "saturate" our souls with God's Word so that no matter what situation comes up in our lives, we can reach into the wellspring of Scripture and apply it to the situation at hand.

Joshua, too, revered the Word of God. When God commanded him to take charge of the Israelite nation, he gave him this wise advice:

> Do not let this Book of the Law depart from your mouth; meditate on it day and night, so that you may be careful to do everything written in it.
>
> Joshua 1:8

Again, the point is driven home. Mind renewal is connected to saturating ourselves constantly with the Holy Writ.

I've always loved Ezra—a man who knew the power of Scripture.

> For Ezra had *devoted* himself to the *study* and *observance* of the Law of the Lord, and to *teaching* its decrees and laws in Israel.
>
> Ezra 7:10

Wow! Think about it. Look how Ezra approached God's holy Word.

- He devoted himself to it.

- He studied it.

- He observed it.

- He taught what he studied and did!

That's a hard combination to beat.

Psalm 119 has 176 verses. I'm amazed as I go through these and realize how many times and in what ways the Word of God is mentioned.

Just look at some of what the Word does for us.

- keeps us pure (v. 9)

- enables us not to sin (v. 11)

- brings calmness (v. 23)

- brings delight (v. 24)

- prevents selfishness (vv. 35–36)

- enables me to withstand pain (v. 61)

- produces endurance (v. 92)

- preserves my life (v. 93)

- provides comfort in danger (v. 95)

- imparts wisdom (v. 98)

- provides light for my path (v. 105)

- brings joy (v. 111)

- grants me understanding (v. 144)

- creates a holy awe (v. 161)

- brings peace (v. 165)

- provides sustenance (v. 175)

Those are but a few things God's Word does for me.

Choosing Positive Companions

Mind renewal is also about choosing to be around people of faith and holiness. It's hard for the mind to be renewed in an atmosphere of negativism and impurity.

Dewayne was a relatively new believer and a newlywed. He worked in construction, and needless to say, his workmates, mostly single guys, not only had foul and vulgar mouths but lived their lives drowning in a sea of negativity. They complained about everything—their jobs, their pay, their dates, their health, their cars, their equipment—you name it. It was very hard for Dewayne to be "up" when he came home to his bride in the evenings. I suggested that, since he couldn't change his work environment, he and Suzie join a Bible study group of couples their age. They found one that met on Tuesday evenings, and just being around some positive guys who didn't swear, boast, or gripe, Dewayne was able to cope at work much better and even went on to be "salt and light" in a putrid and dark situation. If we are constantly around negative, immoral, critical people, we tend to be brought down inch-by-inch to their level. Maybe this is why Paul said,

> Do not be misled: "Bad company corrupts good character."
>
> 1 Corinthians 15:33

While we must go to corrupt people in order to share Christ with them, we're better off not to continually socialize with them. If we're forced to work around such people, we need to develop a fellowship of friends who are wholesome, clean, and positive.

Renewal is not a one-time procedure; it's a process that must go on and on. It takes diligence, persistence, consistency, and a strong desire to be what Jesus wants us to be. Continually renewing the mind is essential for those who desire the victorious life. It's easy to fall into defeat if we're not being renewed, revived, refreshed, and reinvigorated by the Holy Spirit.

Enemies of Renewal

That's right; if you attempt to be renewed in the spirit of your mind, you will run into opposition, because Satan doesn't want you renewed. He will use a host of things to keep you from this all-essential process.

A Busy Schedule

When your schedule is jam-packed, it's easy to put off getting into God's Word. Keeping you busy is a trick of the devil to get you off track. Everyone I know who's living the Christian life is busy, but if we're too busy to take time to be alone with God in prayer and the Word, we're too busy.

A Negative Mood

There is enough bad in our world to put anyone in a negative mood. But, as believers, we must continue to believe that we truly are

> *more than conquerors* through him who loved us.
> Romans 8:37

We must continue to believe that the one who is in us is greater than the one who is in the world. We may fall into a negative ditch on occasion, but we don't have to stay there and wallow. Get out of it as quickly as you possibly can.

Bitterness

Bitterness will keep you from the renewal process quicker than anything else. When we withhold forgiveness from others, we give the devil a foothold (Ephesians 4:27). You can't harbor ill will toward others and be victorious.

Selfishness

"If you have been crucified with Christ, stay dead!" I recently saw those words on a bumper sticker. I think you'll agree that there's a message to ponder there. The old "us" has been crucified. But when we put self first, turn inward, and become self-centered, we are defeated by a quickie resurrection of that old self. Egotism and a self-centered attitude will certainly tumble us into the river of defeat every time.

Worldliness

The Bible tells us not to love the world or the things in the world and that friendship with the world makes us enemies of God. Renewal of the mind becomes impossible when we're caught up in worldly pursuits, adopting worldly standards, and buying into the worldly value system.

Anger

I've discovered that anger cancels out any attempt on my part to keep my mind renewed. Exploding, losing my cool, and seething with a mad attitude keep me away from the Word; and without the Word, my mind cannot be renewed.

Thank God that when we became Christians, we were given the righteousness of Christ. God imputes to us a holiness and purity that make us clean in his eyes, but God also wants us to develop a daily, practical purity and holiness; and we'll never do that without renewing our minds.

Prayer

God, help me to be committed to a renewed mind. Keep me in your Word and on my knees, humbly and willingly following you. Let the renewal of my mind be an ongoing process in my life, so that my practice will match my position.

Amen.

Staying Victorious through Worship and Praise

- What worship is
- Why we praise him

  Praise is desired by God

  Praise extols God's worthiness

  Praise is God's purpose in creation

  Praise rightly honors God's holiness

  Praise is the only proper response to our salvation

  Praise underscores our unworthiness

  Praise moves God to manifest himself to us

  Praise releases God's power

FIVE

The Profound Power of Praise

Staying Victorious through Worship and Praise

"Jerry" was single, thirty years old, handsome, charismatic, and seemingly totally devoted to Christ. He came to me expressing a strong desire to go into the ministry—which would entail leaving a lucrative career in electrical engineering. As we talked about the consequences of this drastic life change, he admitted that he was having a very difficult time walking in and living in victory on a consistent basis. He was living in defeat more than triumph. Together, we tried to discover his problem. I asked him the usual questions with no success; finally I asked him what his WQ (Worship Quotient) was. In other words, was he was involved in personal praise and worship, and did he actively praise God in public worship services? Looking down to the floor, Jerry admitted that worship and praise were almost totally absent from his life. Furthermore, he was not really sure of their significance or where they fit in his walk with the Lord.

Jerry is not alone. It's estimated that up to one half of all who attend an evangelical church on Sundays do not worship publicly or privately. I laid out some principles for Jerry, and he went to work. In about one month I received a note in the mail signed, "Worshiping and happy, Jerry!"

Satan does everything he can to steal worship from the church's life. He knows that if he can strip the church of its emphasis on worship, he can strip the church of its power.

Someone has said that the purpose of the church is *worship, Word, witness,* and *work*—in that order!

Unless worship is in its proper place, preaching the Word, witnessing to others, and working in the body of Christ matter very little.

What Worship Is

Someone has said that worship is "Giving God goose bumps!" That definition presupposes that God not only seeks our worship, but thoroughly enjoys it. From reading Scripture, I think that is absolutely right.

Worship is . . .

- the summation of adoration

- the beholding of God's greatness

- the expression of our highest congratulations

- the singing of our noblest songs

- the extension of our deepest appreciation

- the conveyance of our greatest compliment

- the bestowing of our finest and best praise

- the most powerful endorsement our soul can offer

- the acknowledgment of God's infinite and eternal worth

- the most selfless act of the human spirit

- the recognition of God's transcendent awesomeness

- the celebration that sets God apart as holy

- the exaltation of God, not us

- the effort to accord all glory to God and none to us

- the blessing of God, asking nothing in return

- the magnification of God and minimization of self

- the giving of our all, asking nothing in return

- the celebration of all celebrations

One golden truth runs through all the definitions of worship: Worship is that special act, done by us to exalt, glorify, magnify, and honor God exclusively.

Why We Praise Him

Worship isn't for us; it's for him. While we are blessed beyond measure in the act of worship, it's end object is God, not us. Understanding *why* we praise God will help us in our practice. There are many reasons, but here's a few.

Praise Is Desired by God

While God has no needs because of his nature, he does have desires. His top desire is to receive praise and worship from our lips and hearts. Jesus said,

> A time is coming and has now come when the true worshipers will worship the Father in spirit and truth, for they are the kind of worshipers *the Father seeks.*
>
> John 4:23

God actually seeks our worship. When you go into your prayer closet and begin your prayer time by worshiping God, just know that he's been hovering over that place anticipating and desiring your worship. God made it clear in Exodus 20:2–5 that we're not to worship any other gods, and in Exodus 34:14 he tells us that he's a jealous God. God wants us to worship him and him alone.

After Jesus' resurrection from the dead, the disciples "came to him, clasped his feet and worshiped him" (Matthew 28:9). Jesus didn't try to stop them but received their worship because he was God. Psalm 33 tells us,

> Sing joyfully to the Lord, you righteous; it is fitting for the upright to praise him.
>
> Psalm 33:1

We worship because God seeks our worship; it's thus appropriate.

Praise Extols God's Worthiness

We worship God because he alone is worthy of our praise. Worship has been scheduled for him alone.

> Ascribe to the Lord, O mighty ones, ascribe to the Lord glory and strength. Ascribe to the Lord the glory *due* his name; worship the Lord in the splendor of his holiness.
>
> Psalm 29:1–2

Notice that glory is *due* his name. Psalm 48:1 says, "Great is the Lord, and most *worthy* of praise."

We're also reminded of his worthiness in the following passage:

> Great is the Lord and most worthy of praise; his greatness no one can fathom.
>
> Psalm 145:3

God is truly worthy of our praise.

Praise Is God's Purpose in Creation

Why worship? Because it fulfills God's very purpose in creating the world. In the book of Isaiah, God says this about his creation:

> The people I formed for myself that they may *proclaim my praise.*
>
> Isaiah 43:21

God created us *not* that we might be happy, prosperous, or well, but that we might praise him. In other words, our purpose for living is to glorify God. In the following passage, God tells his creation to praise him.

> Let the sea resound, and everything in it, the world, and all who live in it. Let the rivers clap their hands, let the mountains sing together for joy.
> Psalm 98:7–8

Here, all that he has created is commanded to praise him. One only need read Psalm 145 and 148 to discover that God expects to receive praise from the trees, flowers, rivers, mountains, and stars. In a day when many worship nature, we need the reminder that God expects nature to worship him. We're not to worship the creation, but the creator! Everything God made was designed to point back to God in adoration and praise. Even the stones are equipped to cry out if people won't!

Praise Rightly Honors God's Holiness

Our God is a holy God, and worship is the only thing that truly acknowledges that. I'm afraid we don't understand much about the awesome and holy nature of God. We treat even the name of God flippantly. But God's holiness is a serious matter.

I find it very interesting that God tells Moses "to worship at a distance" (Exodus 24:1). In 1 Chronicles 16:28–29 we're told to "worship the Lord in the splendor of his holiness." He's called "majestic in holiness, awesome in glory" in Exodus 15:11, and in Isaiah 57:15 he's called "high and lofty" and "holy." When Isaiah experienced the holiness of God in the temple he said,

> I saw the Lord sitting upon a throne, *high and*
> *lifted up.*
>
> Isaiah 6:1 ASV

It comes as a surprise to a lot of people that the chief reason Moses wasn't permitted to go into the Promised Land was that he didn't uphold God's holiness in front of the people (Deuteronomy 32:51). God is to be worshiped because he's holy and deserves our highest praise.

Praise Is the Only Proper Response to Our Salvation

That's right. We praise him because we're eternally thankful for his salvation in us. We're told in Isaiah 43,

> I am he who blots out your transgressions, for my
> own sake, and remembers your sins no more.
>
> Isaiah 43:25

"For my own sake" means that our salvation is for his glory, not just so we can go to heaven when we die. That's why Paul told the church at Ephesus that our forgiveness and redemption are "for the praise of his glory" (Ephesians 1:6, 12, 14).

In Revelation, we're told that the praise of heaven will sound like this:

> Worthy is the Lamb, who was slain, to receive
> power and wealth and wisdom and strength and
> honor and glory and praise!
>
> Revelation 5:12

What a song! And we can begin singing this heavenly praise here on earth! We worship because of our salvation.

Praise Underscores Our Unworthiness

When Nehemiah finished building the wall of the city, Israel worshiped God, but before they worshiped, they confessed their sins (Nehemiah 9:1–3). Worship of a holy God is virtually impossible without understanding and acknowledging our own unworthiness. After Isaiah saw the greatness and holiness of God in the temple, he saw himself. Only in the pristine presence of a holy and righteous God can we accurately see, in contrast, the shabbiness of our own soiled lives. Job said,

> I am unworthy—how can I reply to you? I put my hand over my mouth.
>
> Job 40:4

Certainly he saw the need to underscore his own unworthiness. When Peter saw the miraculous work of Jesus, he fell at his feet and worshiped him, declaring that he was unworthy (Luke 5:8). What an appropriate response.

Praise Moves God to Manifest Himself to Us

We know that God is omnipresent (everywhere present). In Psalm 139, David acknowledged that no matter where he went, God was already there. While God is everywhere, he's not manifest everywhere. Even scriptural accounts of God's manifestations are few. He manifested himself in the Garden of Eden, at the giving of the covenant to Abraham, in the burning bush, in the pillar of cloud and fire over the tabernacle, on Mount Sinai, and in a special revelation to Moses where he was permitted to see only the back side of God's presence. But the Bible tells of another manifestation that is particularly interesting. When the ark of God was brought from Zion to the City of David, the worshipers

> joined in unison, as with one voice, to give praise and thanks to the Lord. . . . Then the temple of the Lord was filled with a cloud, and the priests could not perform their service because of the cloud, for the glory of the Lord filled the temple of God.
>
> 2 Chronicles 5:13–14

In the Old Testament, such manifestations were called the "Shekinah" glory of God. No one really understands them, but at least here, it was precipitated by the energized worship of God's people, which included a trumpet choir of 120!

Praise Releases God's Power

Praise triggers God's power, intervention, and deliverance. When Shadrach, Meshach, and Abednigo stood by their convictions and honored God, they were not singed in the furnace. It was after Daniel praised and thanked his God that he was spared injury or death in the lion's den. It was after Jehoshaphat praised God that his enemy was routed, and not until. When Jonah completed his song of praise in the belly of the giant fish, he was vomited out on dry land. It was after Paul and Silas sang hymns to God in jail that they were freed and the jailer saved. Praise releases the power and the presence of God in a way that it's not released otherwise.

There are many other reasons to worship God beside the few I've listed; but the question is, How will my worship of God help me stay on the path of victory? The prophet Isaiah provides some insight. In a moving message of God's love for his people, Isaiah said that he had been anointed by God to bestow

> a garment of praise instead of a spirit of despair.
> Isaiah 61:3

The presence of praise means the absence of despair, dejection, discouragement, and despondency.

How can you live triumphantly every day? Develop a habit of praise and worship, not just in church on Sundays, but also in your own private, daily devotions. Here's a little acrostic to help you:

P-roclaim his great attributes.

R-ehearse his great feats in history.

A-scribe to him the glory due his name.

I-nvite his presence to become manifest.

S-ing to him a new song every day.

E-xpress your heartfelt thanks to him.

Remember, we praise God for his own worth and glory. We don't praise to get, yet when we praise we are blessed with a new sense of his power and presence. And there's nothing like God's power and presence to help us live a consistently victorious life!

O Lord, our Lord,
how majestic is your name in all the earth!
You have set your glory
above the heavens.
From the lips of children and infants
you have ordained praise.

Psalm 8:1–2

Prayer

Lord, you alone are worthy of my greatest song and my highest praise. Even if I had a thousand, yea a million tongues, I could not praise you enough, but let my life be consumed with trying! I give you glory, honor, power, dominion, authority, because you alone are worthy; you alone are holy; you alone are entitled to the deepest and highest adoration I could ever utter. Teach me anew that when I glorify you, I horrify Satan. So be exalted, O God, above the heavens, and let your glory fill all the earth.

Amen.

Handling Temptation

- Realize that you're not alone
- Avoid temptation's neighborhood
- Rely on God's Word
- Pray
- Turn and run as fast as you can
- Remember God's wonderful promises
- Beware Satan's attacks on your strong points
- Resist the devil so he will flee
- Remember the source of all temptation
- Affirm that you are no longer a slave of sin

Terrifying the Tempter

Handling Temptation

I'll change his name to Tony, but that's all that's changed. The following facts are true. The phone call was frantic. "Pastor, I'm downtown, but I can be at your office in twenty minutes. May I come right now?" You didn't have to be a voice expert to realize this guy was desperate. I agreed to see him, although I didn't know him or recognize his name. Thirty minutes later, a very handsome, well-dressed, twenty-eight-year-old man sat across my desk and burst into tears.

"I can't go on fooling myself and others . . . I am a sex addict. I can't hide it any longer." The story that followed was almost too bizarre to be true. Tony's activity began when he was only fourteen years old. By the time he was a senior in high school, he had "conquered" dozens of girls, and his two years in college left a string of broken-hearted coeds, three of whom had become pregnant. Now a salesman, Tony shared with me that he was sexually involved three and four times a week—he couldn't seem to stop himself.

He said he had become a Christian when he was twenty-one. But he had received no discipleship or follow up and had slipped back into his old lifestyle within two weeks. Now he hated himself, and was plagued day and night by guilt that wouldn't go away. "The temptations are just too great. There is no way I can say no when confronted with opportunity. I guess I'm doomed."

What I shared with Tony, over several sessions, is what I'm sharing in this chapter.

Satan is called the "tempter" because his goal for your life is to lead you into temptation, take away your desire to resist, and help you plunge headlong into sin (1 Thessalonians 3:5). If you choose to live by your lower nature, you'll fall right into the tempter's hands. Many fail to live the victorious life today, because they don't know how to handle the tempter.

Jesus promised us that temptation to sin is sure to come.

> Things that cause people to sin are bound to come.
>
> Luke 17:1

As long as we're trying to please God, Satan is going to jump in the middle of it all and attempt to lure and entice us to sin. But the big question is still unanswered: *How can we live triumphantly every day and be victorious over temptation?*

I offer the following suggestions to help you terrify the tempter and handle your temptation.

Realize That You're Not Alone

> No temptation has seized you except what is common to man.
>
> 1 Corinthians 10:13

We are prone to feel that we are singled out when it comes to temptation, but the truth is that everybody on earth is tempted in one way or another. No one, Christian or non-Christian, is immune from temptation. It eventually gets to us all. Even the close disciples of Jesus were sorely tempted when Jesus was praying in the garden. Jesus himself was tempted to sin during his forty-day fast. Temptations come to all—you are not alone.

Avoid Temptation's Neighborhood

In other words: Don't play with fire, or you'll get burned. Stay away from situations that tempt you in your weak points. Jesus said,

> The spirit is willing, but the body is weak.
>
> Matthew 26:41

Jesus here acknowledges that we're made up of more than one material! While our spirit has the greatest of aspirations, our bodies are extremely weak and subject to frailty. So the best thing to do is avoid the neighborhood where sin lurks. Tony's problem was that he continually allowed himself to wander into tempting surroundings.

It's like the booze drinker who goes six blocks out of the way so he can "drive by" the tavern or the overeater who walks in the bakery just to "look around." If I have a weakness for ice cream, I shouldn't park in front of the local ice cream shop! If you have a problem with lusting after the opposite sex, stay away from places where sexually alluring people are likely to be.

Rely on God's Word

Studying the wilderness temptation of Jesus provides us with the ammunition we need to terrify the tempter. Satan first tempted Jesus through an appeal to his physical appetite: "If you are the Son of God, tell these stones to become bread" (Matthew 4:3). In response, Jesus whipped out the Word of God and quoted,

> Man does not live on bread alone, but on every word that comes from the mouth of God.
> Matthew 4:4

His second temptation appealed to his ego: " 'If you are the Son of God,' he said, 'throw yourself down.' " Again, Jesus relied totally on Scripture and replied,

> It is also written: "Do not put the Lord your God to the test."
> Matthew 4:7

Finally Satan appealed to his greed: "Again, the devil took him to a very high mountain and showed him all the kingdoms of the world and their splendor. 'All this I will give you,' he said, 'if you will bow down and worship me'"(Matthew 4:8–9). For the third time, Jesus responded with Scripture:

> Away from me, Satan! For it is written: "Worship the Lord your God, and serve him only."
> Matthew 4:10

If Jesus, the very Son of God, used Scripture to fend off the temptations of the devil, can we do less? That's why we need to be in God's Word on a daily basis, storing that Word in our hearts so that we don't sin against God (Psalm 119:11).

Pray

This principle is so simple that we're apt to stumble right over it. In the Garden of Gethsemane, Jesus asked his disciples to watch with him for one hour. Exhausted, they fell asleep. His advice to them was,

> Pray so that you will not fall into temptation.
> Matthew 26:41

Notice that he said, "Pray *so that* . . . you may not fall into temptation." In other words, prayer is an antidote for blatant yielding. I'm not talking about namby-pamby prayer, but gut-wrenching, knee-bending, tear-shedding, agonizing, desperate, do-or-die prayer. When time is of the essence, you might try the simple method a coworker shared with me. She said the way she avoided sin when tempted was to pray, "Lord, I'm tempted to sin. Without your intervention, I'm a goner. Help!" That's pretty basic and elementary, but it worked for her. I think it will work for anyone who sincerely prays.

Turn and Run as Fast as You Can

I'm intrigued by the story of Joseph in the Old Testament. The Bible tells us he was a very handsome young man. One day, Potipher's wife came on to him, inviting him to lay with her. No one would have known. He could have gotten away with it. He was severely tempted. Day after day, her advances got more intense. On one particular occasion, when no one else was in the house, she caught him by the cloak and said, " 'Come to bed with me.' But he left his cloak in her hand and ran out of the house" (Genesis 39:12). Joseph refused to compromise his convictions. He dealt concisely and quickly with sin—he turned from it and *ran*. We need to do the same. Paul wrote to the Corinthians,

> Flee from sexual immorality.
> 1 Corinthians 6:18

The word "flee" means run, escape, abandon quickly. To hang around and play footsie with sin ensures defeat.

Remember God's Wonderful Promises

In 1 Corinthians 10, believers are given two great promises concerning temptation. The first one concerns the severity of temptation that God allows Satan to put on us.

> And God is faithful; he will not let you be tempted beyond what you can bear.
> 1 Corinthians 10:13b

That simply means that the power and allurement of the temptation will never be stronger than the resources you have to overcome it. No, not by your own strength, but through the strength Christ provides by his very presence in your life. In the words of Ian Thomas, "I can't, Lord, but you never said I could; you can, and you always said you would!" Rest assured that no matter how powerful and magnetic the temptation, the power within you is always greater. You only have to tap into it and use it.

The second promise is even more exciting. God promises to provide a way of escape.

> But when you are tempted, he will also provide a way out so that you can stand up under it.
> 1 Corinthians 10:13c

There is a way out! When we get lost, it's comforting to know there is a way out. When we're drowning in a sea of financial debt, it's good to know there is a way out. By the same token, when confronted by strong and powerful temptation, knowing that God has provided a way of escape helps us "stand up under it." There is an escape route!

Beware Satan's Attacks on Your Strong Points

Satan is creative and sneaky! We expect him to attack our weak areas, but sometimes he catches us off guard by attacking us at our strong points. Remember how he caused Peter to fall? He attacked Peter where he thought he was strong—in his ability to command leadership, to be the hero, the star! Peter boldly told the Lord, "I'll never forsake you." But Satan used that. His strength became his weakness.

Remember Job? Satan trapped him in his integrity, his strongest spiritual asset. Job thought so much of his integrity that it became his pride, and it was at that point that Satan got him. It was Samson's strength that Satan used to bring him down. Beware that your strength doesn't become a bridgehead for sin.

Resist the Devil so He Will Flee

I'm simple enough to take the promises of the Bible at face value. But God's promises are often preceded by commands. Such is the case in James:

> Resist the devil, and he will flee from you.
> James 4:7

Note: James didn't say *listen* to the devil or *argue* with the devil or *reason* with the devil but *resist* the devil. I believe we need to verbally speak to the devil out loud when confronted with evil and sin: "Satan, I resist and rebuke you in Jesus' name. I renounce your influence and defy your attempt to lure me into sin. My answer is no!"

Remember the Source of All Temptation

Some people have the idea that God tempts them to see how strong they are. Nothing could be farther from the truth. While God may allow us to go through various trials that test the fiber of our faith, nowhere in Scripture are we told that God gangs up on us and tempts us.

Satan, the tempter, is the one who does the tempting. Jesus' wilderness temptation began when "the *tempter* came to him" (Matthew 4:3). Paul wrote to the Thessalonians,

> I was afraid that in some way the *tempter* might have tempted you.
>
> 1 Thessalonians 3:5

The most powerful and convincing Scripture on this subject is found in James.

> When tempted, no one should say, "God is tempting me." For God cannot be tempted by evil, nor does he tempt anyone.
>
> James 1:13

This clearly tells us that God is not in the tempting business. In fact, James goes on to say,

> Each one is tempted when, by his own evil desire, he is dragged away and enticed. Then, after desire has conceived, it gives birth to sin; and sin, when it is full-grown, gives birth to death.
>
> James 1:14–15

In *The Message* translation, Eugene Peterson vividly translates the above passage this way.

> The temptation to give in to evil comes from us and only us. We have no one to blame but the leering, seducing flare-up of our own lust. Lust gets pregnant, and has a baby: sin! Sin grows up to adulthood and becomes a real killer.
>
> James 1:14–15

What James is doing in these verses is showing us the life cycle of sin; and that cycle begins with temptation.

1. Temptation entices.

2. Desire conceives.

3. Sin is birthed.

4. Sin grows up.

5. Sin does its deadly work!

What a downward spiral! When temptation knocks, an enticed hand opens the door, a love affair develops (between us and sin), sin is conceived in us, birth follows, and spiritual death is the outcome. That's a scary scenario. The good news is that you can stop Satan in his tracks by refusing to answer the door when he knocks. But beware: your refusal will infuriate him, and he'll knock even harder the next time. You do have the power inside you not to respond; the question is, Will you use that power? It's up to you.

Hal put his head in his hands as he regretfully told me how he had left his door ajar. He worked in a five-person office—himself, two other men, and two women. He found himself staying after five many evenings to get caught up with accounts payable. Dottie's office was just outside his cubicle, and he began to notice that when he stayed late, she stayed late. One evening she massaged his shoulders to soothe a headache, and he was aroused. Instead of running, resisting, getting up, or walking away, he soaked up every minute. That led to coffee after work at a nearby cafe, a long ride in the car to the country, then ultimately adultery. I marveled as he explained the sequence of events that led to his flagrant sin. He labeled these steps as looking, talking, touching nonsensuous places, intimate talking, embracing, then sex. He was so ashamed, so mad at himself for falling for the seduction of this woman who, he later learned, had seduced one other man in the same office. But it was he who opened the door when sin knocked. You can fight off temptation much easier if you will remember that its source is Satan. The Bible gives us this warning:

> But if you do not do what is right, sin is crouching at your door; it desires to have you, but you must master it.
>
> Genesis 4:7

It's up to us, the ball is in our court when the doorbell of sin rings.

Affirm That You Are No Longer a Slave of Sin

You can't affirm it too many times. In fact, Satan wants you to forget it. But the Bible is clear when it says,

> For we know that our old self was crucified with him so that the body of sin might be done away with, that we should no longer be slaves to sin.
>
> Romans 6:6

Later in that same chapter, Paul reminds us to consider ourselves dead to sin. That means "unresponsive to" sin. In verse 12, he also tells us not to let sin "reign" in our mortal bodies so that we "obey its evil desires." He concludes that section in verse 14:

> For sin shall not be your *master*, because you are not under law, but under grace.
> Romans 6:14

When you surrendered to Christ, your relationship to sin changed. Before you were saved, sin was your master. It told you what to do. It commanded you to answer the doorbell of sin. You were obligated to obey; you were controlled by the master, sin. When sin said "Jump!" you simply said, "How high?" You fully obeyed its commands. But now that you have been saved, your relationship to sin has changed. When you put your faith in the finished work of Christ, a legal transfer of ownership transpired—Jesus purchased you from Satan. You, in turn, transferred your loyalty to a new master.

Now when sin barks its orders, you are no longer obligated to obey. You have a new master, Jesus, and he has given you the power to say *no* to the old master and *yes* to him.

Why do you still sin on occasion? Good question. The answer is simple—you *choose* to. Look at it this way. Suppose there are two fields separated by a fence. The first field is the field of sin. That's where you once lived, without God, without hope, without forgiveness. Then one day you accepted Christ and were placed in a new field—the field of righteousness. Your new position was made possible by the death of Christ on the cross and your faith in it. Living in the new field, you grow and flourish, but then one day you hear a voice from the other field. "Hey, we're having a party! Come on over; once won't hurt.

After all, your old friends are here. Come on; it won't hurt." So, in a weak moment, you yield and jump the fence. In a short time, you realize what you've done and say, "What on earth am I doing back over here? I was delivered from this; this is not where I'm supposed to be." Then you jump the fence again, and you're back in the field of righteousness.

What happened? For a short time, through the allurement of sin, you allowed yourself to be enticed by those voices in the other field, and you went for it. But as you mature in your walk with the Lord, those voices have less and less appeal, and when they call again, you respond, "No way, I live in a new field now and won't go back." Remember, you don't *have* to answer the doorbell of sin and Satan; you now have the power to stay away from the door!

Sometimes I think we Christians need to hang a sign around our necks that reads "Under new management," because, in fact, we are. The Lord Jesus Christ is our new manager, and our whole agenda has changed.

Remember Tony? You'll be glad to know that he began meeting with another man who had been delivered from the same bondage. They met together for about six months; and by his own testimony, Tony is now a new man! Tony learned some things from this man that no one had ever shared with him before. First, he learned that he didn't have to stay enslaved to sin; he learned that he could be set free from that bondage. He also learned that he needed to be accountable to someone who was willing to ask him the hard questions. What about temptation? It's still there, but he now has a passion for victory that outweighs his passion for lusting after the flesh. What Tony found any man can find, through the life-changing principles of God's Word.

You can beat temptation at its own game. You have the desire, God has given you the power, and Satan deserves to hear your resounding *no!* Just do it!

Prayer

O Lord, temptations are so strong, and my resistance is often weak! Indeed, Lord, the spirit is willing, but my flesh is weak. I do not ask you to provide extra power, just wisdom to draw from the limitless supply you've already promised. I'm trusting in your ennoblement, not mine; your direction, not mine; your power, not mine; your commitment never to leave or forsake me. Let any yielding that I do be yielding to your standard and your will.

Amen.

The Place of Prayer in Victory

- What is prayer?
- Occasions when Jesus prayed
- Why pray?
- How do we pray?
  Experience the presence of God
  Praise him, praise him!
  Offer thanksgiving
  Confess your sin
  Petition God
- Enemies of prayer
  Sin
  An unforgiving heart
  Busyness
  Selfishness
  Television

SEVEN

Routine Rendezvous

The Place of Prayer in Victory

We were on our way to a men's retreat in our church bus. Cal sat down next to me. He was in his early thirties, worked as a crane operator, and had gone through a painful, ugly divorce. We weren't five miles into the trip when he said, "I'm glad I got to sit next to you. I'm not staying on top in my Christian walk; in fact, that's why I came to this retreat—I'm looking for something to help."

"Cal," I asked, "how was your prayer time this morning?"

He gave me a blank look. "I didn't have a prayer time this morning."

"Well," I pressed, "how was your prayer time yester-day morning?"

He got a sheepish grin on his face and confessed that he'd been too busy to pray for weeks. I had uncovered the source of Cal's defeat. We had an hour and a half to talk, so I shared with him some of the ins and outs of prayer that I had learned.

I'm impressed that the only thing the disciples ever asked Jesus to teach them was how to pray.

> Lord, teach us to pray.
>
> Luke 11:1

They didn't ask him to teach them to study or serve or win souls, but they asked him to teach them how to pray.

What Is Prayer?

The following definitions will set the stage for this important chapter.

- Prayer does not turn God into a spiritual "genie" we call out of a bottle to do our will and give us what we want.

- Prayer is not wrenching blessings from an unwilling God, rather it is turning on the faucet so God can give what he desired and intended to give all along.

- Prayer is not overcoming God's reluctance, but laying hold of God's willingness.

- Prayer is a means of discovering God's will. We do not pray to get what we want; we pray to find out what God wants from us.

- Prayer is communion with God.

- Prayer is sensing the presence of God.

- Prayer is experiencing the presence of God.

- Prayer is holy breathing in the presence of God.

- Prayer is giving God access to our needs.

- Prayer is a cannonball shot through the gates of heaven and into the throne room of God.

- Prayer is prevailing before him with praise, thanksgiving, and requests.

Occasions When Jesus Prayed

Jesus himself is our prayer model. Have you ever stopped to think of the different occasions on which Jesus felt the need to pray?

- He prayed before he preached (Mark 1:35).

- He prayed when his heart was sad (Matthew 14:13).

- He prayed for strength after ministering to others (Matthew 14:23).

- He prayed before the responsibilities of the day began (Luke 4:42).

- He prayed all night before selecting his disciples (Luke 6:12).

- He prayed with his disciples (Luke 9:28).

- He prayed for the unity of his followers (John 17).

- He prayed a prayer of thanksgiving to God (Luke 10:21).

- He prayed while dying on the cross (Matthew 27:46).

If Jesus, the Son of God, found the time to pray and saw it as a necessity, who am I that I should neglect this high and holy privilege.

Why Pray?

But how does prayer inflame my passion for victory and help me live triumphantly every day? That question is answered by looking at the "why" of prayer. So, why do we pray? Many reasons come to mind.

- Jesus set the example (Mark 1:35).

- Jesus commands it (Matthew 7:7).

- It's the only way to affect some things (Mark 9:29).

- It reveals God's plans for us (Jeremiah 33:3).

- So we won't lose heart (Luke 18:1–8).

- To keep us from temptation (Mark 14:38).

- To affect government (1 Timothy 2:1–2).

- To be healed (James 5:13–15).

- To get divine wisdom (James 1:5).

- To get the world evangelized (Matthew 9:38).

- So we won't sin against God (1 Samuel 12:23).

- So the Holy Spirit can present our requests to God (Romans 8:26).

- To be set free from captivity (Jeremiah 29:11–14).

- To get a sense of direction (Jeremiah 42:3).

- To keep an awareness of God's forgiveness (1 John 1:9).

- To change the behavior of our enemies (Luke 6:28).

- To gain boldness for witnessing (Ephesians 6:19–20).

- To get fellow believers to grow and bear fruit (Colossians 1:10–11).

- For the salvation of our friends and relatives (Romans 10:1).

- To get out of impossible situations (Jonah 2:1–10).

- For the unity of the church (John 17:6–23).

- For the selection of leadership (Acts 13:3).

- For the perfection of the saints (2 Corinthians 13:9).

- To offer a sweet incense to God (Revelation 5:8).

- So God can be hallowed and praised (Matthew 6:9).

- To get the peace of God (Philippians 4:6–7).

Actually, that list could go on and on, but I think we all get the point. We pray for a reason. I like to compare prayer with a kitchen faucet. Inside the faucet, water is waiting to come out. It wants to come out. It's ready to come out. It's pressured to come out. The water is backed up all the way to the main water line that runs down your street. That water line is backed up to the main water line that runs through your end of town, and that is backed up all the way to the reservoir that serves your city. But it will stay in those pipes till you turn the tap! When you do, it will flow in abundance.

There are some things God won't do unless we pray. He is waiting with unlimited power to intervene in areas of our lives that need his special touch. But we must "turn the tap." That tap is prayer.

How Do We Pray?

We're told in 1 Thessalonians 5:17 to pray always. This doesn't mean we're to be on our knees twenty-four hours every day, but it does mean we are to remain in an attitude of communion with a holy God. God created us to have fellowship with him—both through special times set apart for prayer and through a continually prayerful frame of mind. Of the thousands of species of animal and wild life, God created man uniquely to have communion with himself. To fail to commune with God is to deny the very reason we were created. But, *how do we pray?*

Ah, that's the question. That was Cal's question. So, here is the step-by-step way to pray that I shared with Cal.

Experience the Presence of God

> Be still, and know that I am God.
> Psalm 46:10

When you pause to pray, you need to go to a secluded place, away from phones, radios, stereos, and people. The first couple of minutes, you need to be still, clear your mind of the mundane, and think only of God's matchless presence. You don't need to ask for his presence—he's already there; you simply need to affirm it, claim it, and thank him for it.

Praise Him, Praise Him!

> Sing to the Lord, you saints of his; praise his holy name.
>
> Psalm 30:4

Praise is "ascribing to the Lord the glory due his name" (Psalm 96:8). It is blessing him, extolling him, exalting him, worshiping him, and lifting him up. You may want to sing a hymn or song of praise to him. The Bible tells us to sing a "new song" to the Lord—a song that isn't in print, a song that simply comes from our hearts spontaneously (Psalm 96:1). We have no right to ask things of him until we have properly worshiped him and set him apart as holy.

Offer Thanksgiving

> Enter his gates with thanksgiving and his courts with praise; give thanks to him and praise his name.
>
> Psalm 100:4

Thank God for your health, your job, your wife, your husband, your family, your church, your home, your house, your country, your salvation, and above all, Jesus! God loves to be thanked. We live in a thankless land and culture; God surely appreciates it when we take time to just thank him for all he has done and is doing in our lives.

Confess Your Sin

> The sacrifices of God are a broken spirit; a broken and contrite heart, O God, you will not despise.
> Psalm 51:17

> For this is what the high and lofty One says—he who lives forever, whose name is holy: "I live in a high and holy place, but also with him who is contrite and lowly in spirit."
> Isaiah 57:15

> This is the one I esteem: he who is humble and contrite in spirit, and trembles at my word.
> Isaiah 66:2

God desires broken and contrite hearts—hearts that are broken over their own sin. We're told in 1 John 1:9 that we are to confess our sins and that God is faithful and righteous to forgive them. Daily confession of sin does at least three things: it lets God know you're truly sorry for the wrongs you have done; it makes you mindful of your sins, enabling you to experience God's abundant grace again and again; and the awareness of sin that confession brings actually helps you sin less and less.

Petition God

> By prayer and petition, with thanksgiving, present your requests to God.
>
> Philippians 4:6

This is the "asking" time of your prayer experience. In Matthew 7:7, Jesus commands us to ask and promises that we will receive. He wants to be asked. One of the simplest testimonies about prayer in the whole Bible is the brief story of a man named Jabez. We're told in 1 Chronicles 4:9 that he was more honorable than his brothers. Then it says,

> Jabez cried out to the God of Israel, "Oh, that you would bless me and enlarge my territory! Let your hand be with me, and keep me from harm so that I will be free from pain." *And God granted his request.*
>
> 1 Chronicles 4:10

Please count the requests he made in this short prayer. (1) "bless me," (2) "enlarge my territory," (3) "let your hand be with me," (4) "keep me from harm," and (5) keep me "free from pain." Five requests in one short prayer, and God granted his requests! What a great lesson for us.

So, for what do you pray? Pray for your spouse, pray for your purity, pray for your children, pray for the sick, for marriages, for your church, for your minister, for your other loved ones, for the lost, for missionaries, for people in government office, for your neighbors, for world evangelization . . . the list is endless. But be sure to pray for your own victory, your own walk, your own testimony. I need a list for my prayer time. I divide my list by days: I pray for fellow ministers on Mondays, my staff on Tuesdays, the lost on Wednesdays, marriages on Thursdays, missionaries on Fridays, weekend services on Saturday and Sunday. You may want to divide your list differently. The important thing is that you take the time, find a place of solitude, and pray.

Enemies of Prayer

You may as well know that prayer has its share of enemies. The old adage is still true: *Satan trembles when he sees even the weakest Christian on his knees!*

How true, how true! Satan doesn't mind your going to church, serving on committees, singing in the choir, teaching a class, or even going to a prayer meeting now and then. He just doesn't want you to get serious about prayer. He doesn't want you to see prayer as an essential in your life. So he has set up some hindrances. What are they?

Let's begin the list with the obvious things, then move to the more subtle.

Sin

> Your iniquities have separated you from your God; your sins have hidden his face from you, so that he will not hear.
>
> Isaiah 59:2

We need to take this warning seriously! When we come into God's presence, we come into the presence of holiness. Unconfessed sin and sin that is unrepented of blocks prayer's answer.

> Who may ascend the hill of the Lord? Who may
> stand in his holy place? He who has clean hands
> and a pure heart.
>
> Psalm 24:3–4

If you are trapped in a persistent sin, you'll have diffi-
culty praying.

An Unforgiving Heart

If you are harboring a grudge, nursing a grievance, or
holding a bitterness against someone, your prayer life
will be hindered. Jesus said,

> For if you forgive men when they sin against you,
> your heavenly Father will also forgive you. But if
> you do not forgive men their sins, your Father
> will not forgive your sins.
>
> Matthew 6:14–15

God will not forgive an unforgiving heart. Maybe this
is why Peter wrote in 1 Peter 3:7 that husbands need to
live considerately with their wives lest their prayers be
hindered.

Broken relationships are definitely enemies of prayer.
That's why Paul advocated we never go to bed angry
(Ephesians 4:26). This is nowhere more applicable than in
our marriages.

Busyness

Most of us have hectic schedules. We get up early, go to
bed late, and still we seem to lag behind. On more than
one occasion, Jesus drew his disciples away to a lonely

place to pray—away from the noise, the hustle, the bustle, the harried schedules. We need to do the same.

Some equate spirituality with how many times they're "down at the church" during the week. "Religious" busyness is one of the most subtle enemies of prayer, because we think of it as "serving the Lord." In some circles, busyness has become a substitute for prayer.

Selfishness

James 4:3 tells us we ask and do not receive because we ask with wrong motives—we ask for things to spend on our own pleasures. Some people see God as a genie who does our bidding for our own purposes. But God will not answer selfish prayers. Ours has become a narcissistic culture with an emphasis on *me*. In fact, much of modern Christianity seeks to entertain believers rather than edify them and challenge them to ministry.

We can become so self-centered and self-conscious that we hinder our own prayers. Real prayer means humbling myself before the Lord, and that is impossible if I'm concentrating on *my* needs, *my* desires, *my* well-being, *my* agenda.

Television

I'm sorry to say, but the average American watches TV 16.7 hours per week. If that's average, some watch it much, much more. One man recently told me he watches the tube some twenty-four hours per week! I could hardly believe it. Should I watch TV more than I frequent my prayer closet? Should my mind absorb what comes through the tube (much of which is garbage) more than it absorbs the Lord's presence? Television keeps many people up late at night, who in turn can't get up early enough in the mornings to have their time alone with God. It is definitely an enemy to prayer.

P rayer is work. It is a discipline. It doesn't come easily. You don't *have* time to pray, you must *make* time to pray. It must be a priority in your life. Nothing will make your passion for victory more a reality than a good prayer life.

I recommend that you pray in the mornings, no matter how early you have to get up. Start your day with God. Don't try to do serious praying just before you go to bed. Chances are, you'll fall asleep.

How vital is prayer to the victorious life? It isn't vital at all; it's absolutely *essential!*

Cal got back to a daily prayer time. Though not every day was super, prayer rekindled his passion for victory and gave him the power he needed to fight off the temptations that plague a single guy in his thirties. He's walking in victory today, but it's because he paid the price for discipline in prayer. How about you? How's *your* prayer life?

Remember Paul's admonition:

> Pray continually.
>
> 1 Thessalonians 5:17

Prayer

Lord, it's so easy to moralize about prayer . . . so difficult to actually do it. You desire communication with me, Lord, more than I desire it with you. Renew my passion to pray and wait. Save me from insane busyness that keeps me from the prayer closet. Remind me again that all is indeed vain unless I pray! Convict me of the fact that nothing eternally significant will occur unless I pray. Lord, let me be a person of prayer, and help me consider time with you the most coveted part of my day.

Amen.

Christian Service in the Body of Christ

- **Principles of service**

  The less we serve, the farther we move
  from victory

  Jesus is our example

  Service to others is also service to
  Christ

  The results of service are not always
  immediate

  Our service will be rewarded in heaven

  All of God's people are called to serve

- **A servant's inventory**

EIGHT

Soaring by Serving

Christian Service in the Body of Christ

I'll call them Trudy and John. I was called to the hospital where their son was seriously ill with a high fever that wouldn't come down. After prayer, we went to the waiting room; Trudy broke the silence. "Pastor, we haven't been as regular in our church attendance as we used to be, and we feel so guilty about it. We feel ourselves slipping in so many areas. We used to have such a passion for victory. We just can't figure out why we feel so weak in our faith."

We talked awhile, and finally I asked them, "Are you serving anywhere in the church?" They both looked at the floor, then reluctantly admitted that they hadn't served in the church for almost two years. John used to be an usher and at one time had driven one of our buses for retreats and camps. Trudy had worked with our preschoolers and had been a regular greeter. She had also helped coordinate funeral dinners for us. Both had been vitally involved in serving. The tender spot had been revealed!

So I shared some time-honored principles about serving with John and Trudy, and I think they're worth sharing with you.

Principles of Service

The Less We Serve, the Farther We Move from Victory

This is demonstrated in a little experiment. The next time you're grilling hamburgers on your deck or in your backyard, pick up one of the red-hot coals with a tong and set it aside on a rock somewhere. Come back in fifteen minutes and look at it, then look at the other coals. The coal you took out will be cold, dark, and incapable of cooking anything. The other coals will still be glowing and cooking the meat! Lesson? It's clear. If you remove yourself from other believers in fellowship and serving, you, too, will grow cold. If you're not involved in serving others, with others, you'll become a spiritual hermit, and you'll lose your heat and influence.

No Christian is a "soloist" or an island unto himself. We were created in Christ Jesus to work closely with one another. Failure to do so will quench our passion for victory and lead us toward defeat.

Only a few years back, I read of a church in Texas that decided to keep a profile for an eighteen-month period of everyone who dropped out of their membership. An astounding 94 percent of those who left had not been involved in any kind of serving or ministry for a year! Does that tell you anything? If the facts were known, I would venture to say that the "victory level" of those people was significantly low as well.

Jesus Is Our Example

When we become disciples of Jesus Christ, we are enroute to becoming "like" him.

> A student is not above his teacher, but everyone who is fully trained will be like his teacher.
> Luke 6:40

Wow! Jesus wants to reproduce himself in *us!* If we want to be like our teacher, we most definitely must learn to serve. Service was the hallmark of Jesus' earthly ministry.

> The Son of Man did not come to be served, but to serve, and to give his life as a ransom for many.
> Matthew 20:28

Christ didn't come to sit on a chair and be served by his disciples; to the contrary—he served *them*, thus leaving us an example to follow. He never asked his disciples to do what he was unwilling to do. Isaiah referred to him as the "suffering servant"; and if we want to be like him, we, too, must learn to serve others.

> Whoever wants to become great among you must be your servant.
>
> Matthew 20:26

True greatness, according to Jesus, is not measured by how much money you have, what kind of position you have, how many people you have under you, or the titles the world has given you. True greatness is found in humbly serving others.

Service to Others Is Also Service to Christ

Jesus taught it; the Bible talks about it. Though it defies full understanding, this principle is true: Service to others is service to Christ.

In the parable of the sheep and the goats, Jesus described the judgment scene as a separation of the righteous and the unrighteous; and the determiner of their destiny was *service*. Jesus told the righteous that they had served him in many ways: when he was thirsty, they had given him a drink; when he was hungry, they had given him food; when he was a stranger, they had invited him in; when he was naked, they had clothed him; when he was in prison, they had visited him; and when he was sick, they had cared for him. But the righteous were shocked. "When did we do these things to you?" That's when Jesus dropped the principle on them:

> I tell you the truth, whatever you did for one of the least of these brothers of mine, you did for me.
>
> Matthew 25:40

Maybe that is why Paul wrote,

> Whatever you do, work at it with all your heart,
> as working for the Lord, not for men, since you
> know that you will receive an inheritance from
> the Lord as a reward. It is the Lord Christ you are
> serving.
>
> > Colossians 3:23–24

So many people who serve the Lord in their local churches get bent out of shape because they don't get recognition or because they have a difference with someone else or because they feel they aren't appreciated by others—and then they quit! How tragic. They forget that their service to others is ultimately service to Christ.

The Results of Service Are Not Always Immediate

We have become a "see-the-results-now" generation, and if we don't see the results immediately, we quit. Perhaps Paul's plea to the Galatians reflects a similar attitude in them:

> Let us not become weary in doing good, for at the
> proper time we will reap a harvest if we do not
> give up.
>
> > Galatians 6:9

Paul speaks of a "proper time." The proper time may not be now. I remember spending almost fifteen hours over a three-month period with a man, trying to convert him to Christ. The results were zero. Almost five years later, that man called to tell me that he had become a Christian and was serving the Lord where he now lived. I nearly fell out of my chair! Five years later! The harvest doesn't always come soon. Sometimes it comes later—sometimes, *much* later. Lack of immediate results should never deter us from serving. We must not become weary in well-doing.

Maybe it's been awhile since you held a responsibility in your local church, and maybe you stopped serving because you just couldn't see any results. I can understand. I've had the same feelings, yet Scripture promises results.

> My word . . . will not return to me empty, but will accomplish what I desire.
>   Isaiah 55:11

That is a very comforting Scripture for all who serve, for God has promised that we will "reap a harvest if we do not give up" (Galatians 6:9). It's our job to serve; the results department is headed up by God!

Our Service Will Be Rewarded in Heaven

That's right, the Bible teaches that our service will be rewarded someday in heaven. While our works have no direct bearing on our salvation—for we are saved by Jesus alone, by grace through faith—our works of service will be put to the test: the Bible calls it a test of fire.

> If any man builds on this foundation using gold, silver, costly stones, wood, hay or straw, his work will be shown for what it is, because the Day will bring it to light. It will be revealed with fire, and the fire will test the quality of each man's work. If what he has built survives, he will receive his reward.
>   1 Corinthians 3:12–14

On a more somber note, Paul said,

> So then, each of us will give an account of himself to God.
>
> Romans 14:12

In Romans, Paul discusses the believers' judgment and says,

> God will give to each person according to what he has done.
>
> Romans 2:6

Paul spoke also of the "crown of righteousness" for all who love the Lord's appearing (2 Timothy 4:8). Maybe you're saying, "Oh, I'm not interested in crowns or rewards; I just want to go to heaven." But think again. God is very interested in the crowns, rewards, congratulations, and honors that he has prepared for those who love and serve him.

I really believe that reward is one of the motives God gives for serving him. Of course, we obey and serve Christ because we love him, but we also serve because he has promised rewards. I believe that if God provides those rewards, he wants us to expect them—not that rewards are our only motivation for doing good—but they are one motivation.

All of God's People Are Called to Serve

God's plan is that every believer in the body of Christ be a server; that's the will of God—no exceptions! Paul put it like this:

> It was he who gave some to be apostles, some to
> be prophets, some to be evangelists, and some to
> be pastors and teachers, to prepare God's people
> for *works of service,* so that the body of Christ may
> be built up.
>
> Ephesians 4:11–12

Please notice this phrase: "to prepare God's people for works of service." God's people—all of them—are to be prepared for works of service. Sacrificial service isn't reserved for special people like Billy Graham and Mother Theresa! It's for *all* his people. It's not "some watch, and some work." No, for those in the body of Christ, it's "all work, obey, serve, and minister." Many evangelicals have drifted into a "spectator" mentality: they come to church to "watch" the performers, pray, and then go home till the next "show." So sad, so sad! That's a far cry from what God intended. When Bud Wilkinson, former Oklahoma University football coach, retired from his position, he was asked by a reporter in Dallas, "What contribution has football made to physical fitness in America?" His answer stunned all. "None," he shot back. "Do you know what football is? It's eleven men on the field who desperately need rest, playing before 75,000 spectators who desperately need exercise." I don't even need to make the application—you have it!

Continuing on in Ephesians 4, Paul says that when God's people are involved in works of service, the church matures. We have a lot of "immature" bodies of believers today because 10 percent of the church is doing 90 percent of the work! If a car operated on only 10 percent of its horsepower, we would rush it to the repair shop or get rid of it.

identifiable information.

We may contact you to provide appointment reminders or information about treatment alternatives or other health-related benefits and services that may be of interest to you.

Any other uses and disclosures will be made only with your written authorization. You may revoke such authorization in writing and we are required to honor and abide by that written request, except to the extent that we have already taken actions relying on your authorization.

You have the following rights with respect to your protected health information, which you can exercise by presenting a written request to the Privacy Officer:

- The right to request restrictions on certain uses and disclosures of protected health information, including those related to disclosures to family members, other relatives, close personal friends, or any other person identified by you. We are, however, not required to agree to a requested restriction. If we do agree to a restriction, we must abide by it unless you agree in writing to remove it.

- The right to reasonable requests to receive confidential communications of protected health information from us by alternative means or at alternative locations.

- The right to inspect and copy your protected health information.

- The right to amend your protected health information.

- The right to receive an accounting of disclosures of protected health information.

- The right to obtain a paper copy of this notice from us upon request.

NOTICE OF PRIVACY PRACTICES

(MEDICAL)

THIS NOTICE DESCRIBES HOW MEDICAL INFORMATION ABOUT YOU MAY BE USED AND DISCLOSED AND HOW YOU CAN GET ACCESS TO THIS INFORMATION. PLEASE REVIEW IT CAREFULLY.

The Health Insurance Portability & Accountability Act of 1996 ("HIPAA") is a federal program that requires that all medical records and other individually identifiable health information used or disclosed by us in any form, whether electronically, on paper, or orally, are kept properly confidential. This Act gives you, the patient, significant new rights to understand and control how your health information is used. "HIPAA" provides penalties for covered entities that misuse personal health information.

As required by "HIPAA", we have prepared this explanation of how we are required to maintain the privacy of your health information and how we may use and disclose your health information.

We may use and disclose your medical records only for each of the following purposes: treatment, payment and health care operations.

- **Treatment** means providing, coordinating, or managing health care and related services by one or more health care providers. An example of this would include a physical examination.

- **Payment** means such activities as obtaining reimbursement for services, confirming coverage, billing or collection activities, and utilization review. An example of this would be sending a bill for your visit to your insurance company for payment.

- **Health care operations** include the business aspects of running our practice, such as conducting quality assessment and improvement activities, auditing functions, cost management

We are required by law to maintain the privacy of your protected health information and to provide you with notice of our legal duties and privacy practices with respect to protected health information.

This notice is effective as of _____, 20____ and we are required to abide by the terms of the Notice of Privacy Practices currently in effect. We reserve the right to change the terms of our Notice of Privacy Practices and to make the new notice provisions effective for all protected health information that we maintain. We will post and you may request a written copy of a revised Notice of Privacy Practices from this office.

You have recourse if you feel that your privacy protections have been violated. You have the right to file written complaint with our office, or with the Department of Health & Human Services, Office of Civil Rights, about violations of the provisions of this notice or the policies and procedures of our office. We will not retaliate against you for filing a complaint.

Please contact us for more information:

For more information about HIPAA
or to file a complaint:

The U.S. Department of Health & Human Services
Office of Civil Rights
200 Independence Avenue, S.W.
Washington, D.C. 20201
(202) 619-0257
Toll Free: 1-877-696-6775

Over the years we have developed a very unbiblical concept of the church. I call it the *we/they* concept: *we*, the spectators, watch *they*, the people on the stage. Sorry, but the New Testament teaches that every believer has received at least one spiritual gift.

> Each one should use whatever gift he has received to serve others, faithfully administering God's grace in its various forms.
> 1 Peter 4:10

Notice that Paul said, "whatever gift he *has* received." The issue in this verse is not whether or not you have received a gift, but that you use the one you have received. For a list of those gifts, read 1 Corinthians 12, Romans 12, and again, Ephesians 4.

In 1 Corinthians 12, Paul likens the church to the human body and the individual members to the various parts of the body. His point? All the body parts have a function, and they don't all do the same thing. The hand does something other than the foot, the eye does something other than the ear. Though the functions are different, functioning is normative for the whole body.

The idea behind spiritual gifts is for people to serve and minister in the area of their God-given giftedness. That doesn't mean a person can't volunteer for a task in another area, but it *does* mean that he will function with a great deal more effectiveness if he's operating in the area of his giftedness. For example: two people are teaching adult Sunday School classes. One person's teaching is disjointed, not related to real life, and thus a bit boring. The other person sparkles when he teaches, seems to "connect" with the class, and brings the Bible to life. What's the difference? One has the gift of teaching, and the other simply volunteered to teach because there was a vacancy. So, should the nongifted teacher never teach? There are occasions when he might teach, but he may want to consider ministering in the area of his giftedness for increased effectiveness. That kind of service keeps our passion for victory alive and enables us to walk in triumph.

A Servant's Inventory

I think one of the best ways to find out if you're serving the Lord as you ought is to ask yourself the following questions:

- Am I now involved in a ministry responsibility in my church?

- Am I involved in a ministry responsibility outside my church?

- Am I consistent in serving, and do I stay at my post of responsibility?

- Do I serve with joy?

- Do I serve with good motives, mainly to minister to others?

- Am I serving in the area of my giftedness?

- Do I encourage others in my sphere of influence to serve?

- Do I serve without a constant desire for recognition?

- Do I serve even when I don't feel like serving?

L et's face it, there is a bent in all of us not to serve. We excuse ourselves by saying we're too busy, too tired, too involved, or too inept. It's easier not to serve than it is to serve. But the fact is, as Christians, we have been crucified with Christ (Galatians 2:20), and it really is no longer I who live but Christ who lives in me. That crucifixion was meant to make us dead to self and alive to Christ . . . and to others.

One of the obvious things I have learned in nearly forty years of pastoring churches is that those who serve, who stand by their posts of responsibility and service, who are involved in the life and ministry of the church, are by and large, *not* the people who fall into sin. You might say they are "too busy serving" to be bothered with yielding to very much temptation. I've observed that the more people serve, with a pure and sincere heart, the closer they get to Jesus. And, the closer they get to Jesus, the more consistently they walk in victory.

Perhaps the following poem can help us take an honest look at our "willingness" level. I've searched for years for the identity of its author, but so far have not found it. Nevertheless, the poem is worth sharing.

> I'll go where you want me to go, dear Lord,
> Real service is what I desire.
> I'll help with the songs anytime, dear Lord,
> But don't ask me to sing in the choir.
>
> I'll do what you ask me to do, dear Lord,
> I'd like to see things come to pass.
> But don't ask me to teach girls or boys, dear Lord,
> I'd rather just sit in my class.

I'll say what you want me to say, dear Lord,
A professing church member I'll be.
I'll attend all the socials and teas, dear Lord,
but at Sunday School don't expect me.

I'll do what you want me to do, dear Lord,
I yearn for the kingdom to thrive.
I'll give you my nickels and dimes, dear Lord,
But please don't ask me to tithe.

I'll help where you want me to help, dear Lord,
I want to be John on the spot!
Souls may perish all around me, dear Lord,
But to win one to Thee I could not.

I'll go where you want me to go, dear Lord,
I'll say what you want me to say.
But I'm busy just now with myself, dear Lord,
I'll help you some other day.

Now do not leave me to myself, dear Lord,
I'll need you so badly, I know.
I will have to take time to die, dear Lord,
After that, Oh, *where will I go?*

Enough said? Enough said! But one more thing *must* be said. We're not saved to sit, we're saved to serve! I'm not a writer of Scripture—that was completed years ago—but if I were, you can believe I would write a verse that said: "He that serveth tendeth to walk in victory; he that serveth not walketh in defeat!"

Serve the Lord with gladness!
                    Psalm 100:2 RSV

Prayer

Father, coming to church and listening is so easy, but change me from a consumer to a producer. Show me how to serve and fill me with a desire to serve you and others. I pray for your wisdom to direct me into service that fits my gifts, that blesses others, that honors you, and that accomplishes success for the Kingdom. When others think of me, let them think of a servant, not a celebrity.

Amen.

Spiritual Warfare

- ## Spiritual warfare 101
  The Christian life is a battleground, not a
  playground
  The battle is not ours, but God's
  Our weaponry is different from the world's
  We must appropriate what we have
  We must understand who the real enemy is

- ## The Christian's armor
  The belt of truth
  The breastplate of righteousness
  The shoes of the gospel of peace
  The shield of faith
  The helmet of salvation
  The sword of the Spirit

- ## The Christian's plan of attack
  Recognize Satan's game plan
  Fight back with the Word of God
  Start a "prayer conspiracy"
  Verbalize your resistance to Satan
  Keep your life pure and clean

Wielding Those Weapons

Spiritual Warfare

Teresa and Devin (not their real names) were three-year-old believers. A young couple, they didn't have a lot of resources, but seemed determined to open their own pharmaceutical shop—they even had dreams of someday expanding the shop into a fully stocked drug-store. Devin's parents provided most of the capital, and they took out a small business loan. The whole project was bathed in prayer—not only by them, but by their whole Sunday school class and Bible study group. They really believed this was God's will for their future, which included possibly going to the mission field in a medical capacity. The day finally arrived for the grand opening.

By the end of opening day, Satan had his plan well under way, and for the next nine months, Teresa and Devin found themselves intimidated and harassed by the enemy. Some of the bullets included the following: The state wrongly fined them for improperly applying for a business license; an employee filed an unfounded discrimination litigation against them, claiming she was treated poorly because of her Jewish background; they were robbed three times, and the third time, their insurance company refused to pay; one of their major suppliers refused to service them because of the "religious" signs they displayed in their shop; five regular customers took their prescriptions elsewhere, because they were offended by the soft Christian music playing in the background and claimed the owners were trying the "cram religion down the throats of their customers." That's not the end of the list. Their non-Christian landlord had cleverly worded the rental contract so he could raise their rent by almost 35 percent. Attack, after attack, after attack!

Teresa and Devin were wearing down. "What do we do? How can we fight back?" It was time to expose them to Spiritual Warfare 101, in the University of Christian Living. Partly because they were relatively new believers and partly because no one had ever explained it to them, they were totally unaware of Satan's desire to ruin them. They didn't know that the moment they decided to be fully devoted followers of Jesus Christ, Satan had opened a file on them with plans to squelch their passion for victory and undo their walk and witness. After a few sessions, plus a little homework, Teresa and Devin were "ready for battle." The rest is history. I don't mean they never had any more problems, but they did learn how to fight back—God's way.

I believe many people are sincerely trying to live the Christian life today by merely going to church, going to Bible study, praying, and having their devotions. All those things are necessary and helpful, but without knowledge that we are at war, they become sitting ducks again and again for Satan's missiles and artillery.

So, how do we fight such a powerful enemy? Let's start with the basics of Spiritual Warfare 101.

Spiritual Warfare 101

The Christian Life Is a Battleground, Not a Playground

Before we can fight our enemy, we must know that *we are at war!* We're soldiers, not tourists! Becoming a Christian did not ensure that your life would be free of friction, opposition, and harassment. In fact, the opposite is true. The Bible tells us to expect opposition and persecution. It's part of the package.

> In fact, everyone who wants to live a godly life in Christ Jesus will be persecuted.
>
> 2 Timothy 3:12

The Christian life is no playground. Our enemy is real, and he is hot on our trail.

> Be self-controlled and alert. Your enemy the devil prowls around like a roaring lion looking for *someone* to devour.
>
> 1 Peter 5:8

Don't let that "someone" be *you!*

Paul understood that our life is a battle, and in 1 Timothy, he told his "true son in the faith" to fight the good fight of faith (1 Timothy 6:12). Then in 2 Timothy, when Paul had come to the end of his life and was able to see it in retrospect, he saw that it had been filled with one battle after another, and he was able to say,

> I have fought the good fight.
>> 2 Timothy 4:7

Take Paul's words as a personal challenge to fight the battles of your life so that in the end you can say with him, "I have fought the good fight!"

The Battle Is Not Ours, but God's

When Jehoshaphat was facing a lethal enemy, he called on the Lord for help, and he was comforted by the words of Jahaziel,

> The battle is not yours, but God's.
>> 2 Chronicles 20:15

Jahaziel also told Jehoshaphat, "You will not have to fight this battle" (v. 17). How comforting to know that when the enemy attacks, it's really not our battle to fight, but God's; and he has promised to go before us, to protect us, to guard us, and to defend us to the very end.

Our Weaponry Is Different from the World's

Devin and Teresa were getting nowhere because they didn't yet know that to be successful in their "fight," they had to use different weapons than their enemy was using. Paul clears this up for us:

> For though we live in the world, we do not wage war as the world does. The weapons we fight with are not the weapons of the world. On the contrary, they have divine power to demolish strongholds.
>
> 2 Corinthians 10:3–4

Our weapons have warheads unknown to the enemy. They have volatile power inaccessible to Satan and his minions. Our weapons are greater than his.

World War II ended when the U.S. dropped the atomic bomb on Nagasaki and Hiroshima, Japan. Historians tell us the war was won literally by a "greater power." The Japanese did not have the power the U.S. had and, thus, lost the war. By the same token, Satan will lose the battle if we are willing to use divine weapons. On the other hand, if we deploy only conventional weaponry, we will lose the battle every time. Japan couldn't fight nuclear weapons with conventional weapons, and we can't fight satanic power with weapons of the world. Unless our measures are divine, we don't have a chance of beating the devil at his game.

We Must Appropriate What We Have

Having the right weaponry and using the right weaponry are two different things. Ray Stedman used to tell about a man who had bought a new car. His neighbor asked him how he liked it. "Fine, but it sure takes a lot of energy to push it everywhere I go." When the neighbor lifted the hood and showed him the engine, the man was ecstatic! Many believers are exhausted because they are "pushing" so hard, not taking advantage of what they already have by virtue of being in Christ.

That's why Paul said,

> Put on the full armor of God so that you can take your stand against the devil's schemes.
> Ephesians 6:11

God has provided us with the armor, but we have to "put it on." In other words, appropriate it. We may have the right weapons and the right armor, but we will lose the battle if we don't use them.

We Must Understand Who the Real Enemy Is

For a long time, Devin and Teresa thought this array of people who were coming after them was the enemy. Not so; they were only the pawns of the enemy. Paul nailed this truth down tightly when he said:

> For our struggle is not against flesh and blood, but against the rulers, against the authorities, against the powers of this dark world and against the spiritual forces of evil in the heavenly realms.
> Ephesians 6:12

No one really grasps exactly what Paul is talking about here, but most believe he's talking about a matrix system of demons, minions, and special agents of Satan. The flesh and blood people who oppose us, harass us, discriminate against us, and persecute us are only instruments of the enemy. It's easy to forget this and come down hard against our fellow humans, when in essence they're just carrying out the will of Satan. These pawns of Satan are actually victims of the enemy, not the enemy itself.

The Christian's Armor

Now that we understand some of the basic truths about this war we're fighting, it's time to strap on our armor. In Ephesians 6:14–17, Paul clearly identifies the pieces of our armor. Let's list them one by one.

The Belt of Truth

Paul says we're to buckle the belt of truth around our waists. The truth is a powerful defense for at least three reasons: (1) it "sets us free" (John 8:32); (2) Jesus is called "the truth" (John 14:6); and (3) God's "word is truth" (John 17:17).

We begin our stance against the evil one by standing on those truths that don't change. We stand on the truth (1) that Jesus is the Christ, the Son of the living God (Matthew 16:16); (2) that he that is in us is greater than he that is in the world (1 John 4:4); (3) that Christ did rise from the dead on the third day (Luke 24:5–7); and (4) that he will never leave or forsake us (Hebrews 13:5). In other words, we stand upon the truth of God's integrity and his Word as we fight the enemy.

The Breastplate of Righteousness

The most vulnerable place on the body is the chest. If only one arrow pierces your heart, you're history. So part of our armor is the breastplate of righteousness. That means that when we were saved, the righteousness of

Christ was transferred to us. Affirm this righteousness; stand on it; wear it; believe it. Satan cannot do us lethal harm as long as we are protected by Christ's righteousness. Satan cannot pierce our salvation. Keep that breastplate on the front burner of your life to remind you of that fact. Wear it to protect your heart.

The Shoes of the Gospel of Peace

In verse 15, Paul says,

> Stand firm . . . with your feet fitted with the readiness that comes from the gospel of peace.

A Roman soldier's boots were of utmost importance—especially in hand-to-hand combat. If he lost his footing, he lost the battle. Paul says our "footing" is the gospel, the good news by which we were saved. We need to revel in the gospel, rejoice in it, thank God for it, and realize that it is still "the power of God for salvation" (Romans 1:16).

The Shield of Faith

A soldier's shield in the first century was all important. With it, flaming arrows were quenched and poisoned arrows were deflected. Paul talks of the flaming arrows of the evil one that come to "burn" us. A life of faith is necessary to win the war—not faith in faith, but faith in the Lord to go before us. It's the kind of faith that believes God over circumstances. It's the kind of faith that gives victory, because we're trusting in the Lord, not us.

The Helmet of Salvation

Helmets protect our heads. That's where our brains are located; our eyes, noses, mouths, and ears are all there too. Knock the head out of operation, and you've mortally wounded the solider. Paul says our covering is *salvation*. The Greek word comes from "salvage." We have been salvaged from the junk heap of sin and given worth and covering by God. The Bible is clear about the fact that our salvation in Christ is made secure by the sure word of Christ himself: "No one can snatch them out of my hand" (John 10:28). As we fight, we need to make sure that our helmet of salvation is on—not that we lose our salvation and have to put it back on—but "on" in the sense of being *aware* that we are eternally secure in Jesus Christ.

The Sword of the Spirit

> Take . . . the sword of the Spirit, which is the word of God.
>
> Ephesians 6:17

When Jesus was tempted, he took out his sword (God's Word) and slashed the devil to pieces. I read recently about a woman in Chicago who was accosted by a robber who demanded her purse and car keys. She responded by quoting Scripture. The robber covered both ears and demanded that she stop, but she kept on quoting. He ran, but was caught, and later said that those words were so powerful they took all the strength out of him. Her words reminded him of sitting in Sunday School as a little boy. Don't tell me Scripture isn't powerful. Scripture is the only offensive weapon mentioned here.

I've tried to make a habit of putting on the whole armor of God every morning before my feet hit the floor. I picture myself buckling on the belt of truth, snapping on the breastplate of righteousness, grabbing the shield of faith, slipping on the helmet of salvation, and finally gripping the sword of the Spirit, God's Word. It's an exercise I believe God wants every Christian to go through daily. It works.

Devin and Teresa began to assume the authority God had given them. While they responded to their attackers in love, they aggressively began to do spiritual warfare against the devil. They won every time. The Bible tells us that the devil is a thief. Among the things he wants to steal from you is the set of weaponry God says is rightfully yours. Don't let him have it. Utilize your God-given artillery! Don't be the victim, be the victor in Jesus' name!

The Christian's Plan of Attack

When you sense that you're under attack by the enemy, how can you fight against him? Here's a step-by-step plan that's both practical and possible.

Recognize Satan's Game Plan

Satan desires to draw you away from your trust in the Lord. He will do this by intimidation, confusion, frustration, fear, discouragement, suspicion, anger, paranoia, and a host of other things. If one doesn't work, he'll back up, shift gears, and come at you again. Remember, he doesn't want you to be a victorious believer. He wants you *defeated.*

Fight Back with the Word of God

That's how Jesus won the battle in the wilderness when he was tempted by the devil. He fought back with the power and authority of God's Word. Three times (answering the three temptations) Jesus said, "It is written." Satan doesn't fare well under the assault of God's holy Word. Don't trust your own word; rely on his Word. That's why it is so very essential to memorize large blocks of Scripture, so we'll have it when the attacks come. (Note: I said "when" the attacks come, not "if" they come—for come they will.)

Start a "Prayer Conspiracy"

What is a "prayer conspiracy"? It's getting a few people to storm the gates of heaven on your behalf—focusing in on the one issue that Satan is trying to use to derail you. God has given us this tool and privilege; we're suckers not to use it. Believe me when I say, prayer seriously affects the enemy's designs on you. It works.

Verbalize Your Resistance to Satan

I've found this to be very effective in my own life. The Bible says,

> Resist the devil, and he will flee from you.
> James 4:7

What does that mean? I think it means fighting offensively, not just defensively. It means taking the initiative. I know a woman whose husband was divorcing her. She had tried through three different attorneys to get him not to file that divorce. He filed anyway. The day before the divorce was to be final, she said, "Pastor, what do I do? I've prayed and prayed. I've pleaded with him, begged him—I don't know what else to do."

I asked her who she thought was behind this whole marriage breakup. It didn't take her long to respond. "The devil," she said decisively.

I urged her to stand up to the devil, oppose him, resist him, and tell him so. This is what she said: "Satan, you're a thief, trying to steal my husband from me. You're a liar, convincing him that divorce is the answer. You're a roaring lion, tearing apart what God has put together. You're a deceiver, blinding the eyes of my husband to what is right. I stand against you today and against all you stand for. I resist all your efforts to destroy my marriage. I command you in Jesus' name to leave the premises of my husband's apartment. I demand that you withdraw the confusion you've brought to him about his love for me. I curse you in the name of Jesus Christ and call you off my marriage once and for all."

After a time of prayer, she left my office at peace. I got a phone call one week later, and she told me that five hours before the divorce was to be final, her husband canceled the proceedings! After working through some problems, they're back together and madly in love.

Will that work every time? I don't know, but it worked for Shirley.

All of us need to stand up to the devil every way we can. In fact, I believe you and I need to proclaim the following mandate to Satan:

> Satan, take note and listen well! Get off my back! You will not conquer me. I'm blood-washed, Spirit-filled, daily delivered, strongly

sanctified, Spirit-soaked, and Word-indwelt. I am linked with sovereign and eternal power and have set my face.

You're a deceiver, but you won't deceive me; you're a liar, but you won't convince me; you're a killer, but you won't murder me; you're a roaring lion, but I'm not devourable; you're subtle, but I'm on to your ways! You parade as an angel of light, but I walk in a brighter light. Your days of deception are over with me. I won't be deceived, detoured, derailed, distorted, distracted, discouraged, or disillusioned by your schemes. Your vile influence won't cross the "No Trespassing" sign on the door of my heart. My life is off-limits to you. My door is closed to you forever! You won't walk in, crawl in, slither in, sneak in, pry in, jump in, swim in, fly in, drive in, or barge into my life. I have a permanent guest that now lives inside, and he cannot share my temple with you.

You may lure, lie, linger, lurch, laugh, lunge, or leap, but you won't come in. Your days are numbered, your kingdom doomed, your designs dwindling, your evil eroding, your devilishness dissolving, your deceit decaying, your deception diminishing, and your death is dying. Your progress is poisoned, your poison is paralyzed, and your penetration is profitless! Your ultimate victory has been canceled, and soon your show will be over!

You can't trap me with your wares, soil me with your subtlety, or defeat me with your deception. He that is in me is greater than you! Now get

off my property, for the day of your final binding
is not far away! Amen.

Keep Your Life Pure and Clean

Our efforts against Satan are weakened by ungodly living. Many people, living impurely, don't understand why
their lives go from bad to worse. Remember, God's bottom line desire for us is not that we be happy, but that we
be holy. Don't expect to win any battles while living an
unholy life.

C hristians do make mistakes, but Teresa and Devin
were falsely charged—both by the state and by their
disgruntled employee. When they and their attorney got
into the "thick" of the fight, it became very apparent that
they were engaged in spiritual warfare and that obvious
harassment was involved. But through it all, they learned
some important lessons, the chief of which was to put on
the whole armor of God and to wear it in their marriage,
their family, their business, and their social life. Today
they are both strong, involved, and I might add, victorious leaders in their church. They have a greater passion
for victory than ever before, all because they learned that
Christianity is a battlefield and that they are soldiers.

Not all of our problems are attacks from Satan, but
many are. Only a life totally devoted to Jesus Christ and
his Word will survive the raging battles to which we are

all exposed. So remember who the enemy is, and strap on the armor you have in Christ. It can make a difference!

Prayer

O God, we don't wrestle with mere flesh and blood, but with principalities, with powers, with world rulers of this present darkness. Remind me that I'm engaged in war, that I daily live on a battleground, not a play-ground. Grant me the courage to put on the whole armor of God so I can successfully pull down strong-holds and perform great exploits in the power of the Spirit.

Amen.

Witnessing and Winning

- Every believer is a witness for Jesus Christ
- The longer we're saved, the fewer unsaved friends we have
- The easiest kind of witnessing is your personal testimony
- There is an inherent power in the Gospel
- Every believer should pray for the unsaved
- God sovereignly draws people to salvation
- God uses both the witness and the Holy Spirit
- More people come to Christ by the witness of friends than by any other means
- People are lost, doomed, and damned without Jesus Christ!

Gossip That Gospel

Witnessing and Winning

B yron was a man in his late forties. He stopped me one evening after I had delivered a message to men on how to influence their peers for Jesus Christ.

"I'm almost fifty years old, Pastor, and I've never, to my knowledge, been responsible for anyone coming to faith in Christ." Byron went on to tell me how for almost twenty years, since he first accepted Christ, he had been up and down like a yo-yo in his Christian walk. In his words, "I've been from ecstasy to the very bottom of the barrel, and I've spent a lot of time on the bottom." We talked for thirty minutes. Byron had never been mentored or discipled by anyone since accepting Christ; his Christian walk had been one of hit and miss—mostly miss.

If statistics are anywhere near accurate, well over 75 percent of you reading this chapter can easily identify with Byron. You've been consistent in going to church, paying your tithe, maybe even serving on a committee, but to your knowledge, you've never been responsible for leading anyone to a saving knowledge of Jesus Christ. That's not to say you haven't helped many other believers to grow, but your involvement in "obstetrics" has perhaps been zero.

I strongly believe that apart from serving, praising, praying, and basking in your identity, sharing the good news of Jesus Christ keeps us walking in victory as much or more than anything. What I shared with Byron, I gladly share with you. These unchanging principles from Scripture, if observed, will enable you to "bear fruit that lasts" (John 15:16).

Every Believer Is a Witness for Jesus Christ

In Byron's words, "For years, I believed Satan's lie that God expects only the 'gifted' to lead others to Christ . . . only those who are trained for it, like pastors and experts." Byron believed exactly what most Christians believe today—that the work of evangelism is for a special class or group of people in the church who have a propensity for that sort of thing. Many years ago, while pastoring a small rural church in Oklahoma and trying to get our people to witness to others, a crusty old farmer told me, "Preacher, I do the repair work around here, and you do the soul winning, and everything will be fine."

But what does God's Word have to say about that? Just before his ascension back into heaven, Jesus gave us the great commission. It's recorded in various forms in Matthew 28, Mark 16, Luke 24, John 20, and Acts 1. The passage in Acts is very pointed, clear, and all inclusive.

> But you will receive power when the Holy Spirit comes on you; and you will be my witnesses in Jerusalem, and in all Judea and Samaria, and to the ends of the earth.
>
> Acts 1:8

Someone has put it this way: *His last words . . . our first concern.* What God has made primary, we dare not make secondary.

There is nothing in Scripture that even hints that the work of winning the lost is confined to a special group of people. *Every Christian is a witness!* The question is, What kind of witness are you? Are you a sloppy, inefficient, undisciplined witness, or are you an enthusiastic, consistent, and excited witness? The choice is yours. But you don't have a choice as to whether or not you are a witness.

What is a witness? By definition, a witness is someone who testifies to what he or she has seen or heard. In our case, as Christians, we are to bear witness to Christ—who he is, what he's done, and what he's able to do in the lives of others. In the original apostolic church, the work of witnessing was never left to a select few "professionals." It was the work of the whole church. A good example of this is found in Acts 8 where we're told that a great persecution broke out against the church. We're told that everyone scattered, except the apostles. We don't know why the apostles didn't scatter. Maybe they thought it

was better to "hang together" than to "hang separately."
But verse 4 of that chapter says,

> Those who had been scattered preached the word
> wherever they went.
>
> Acts 8:4

Who were the *"those"*? Not the apostles; they didn't
scatter. The "those" were the church. They were plain
people like you and me. Not apostles, not "clergy," not
professionals, not experts, but the church! Oh, I'm sure
the apostles witnessed where they were hanging together,
but what is important here is that the whole church was
witnessing wherever they went—in the marketplace, in
neighborhoods, wherever they happened to be. Satan's
biggest lie is the lie of "specialization" that assigns the
task of witnessing to only a small, select group of people.
If he can get the church to believe that lie, very few will
be won to Christ.

The Longer We're Saved, the Fewer Unsaved Friends We Have

This may not be a biblical principle, but it certainly is a
truth we need to face. When people become Christians,
100 percent of their friends do not know the Lord, or
almost 100 percent. As time goes by, it's only natural that
their new friends are Christians. But I believe that when
new converts are discipled, they need to be taught to
maintain old friendships (as long as those friendships
don't pull them from the Lord) and to develop new

friendships with those who aren't saved. Otherwise, how will we ever influence others?

I know a man who regularly plays racquetball, as many as two or three times per week. He makes a practice to play *only* with non-Christian men, just so he can cultivate relationships that become an entree to sharing Christ. It would be easier to play with his Christian brothers, but as he says, "I need to influence non-Christian guys more than I need to influence Christian guys." Good point.

The Easiest Kind of Witnessing Is Your Personal Testimony

That evening after the Bible study, I asked Byron to share his personal testimony with me. For a man who had never witnessed to anyone, I was amazed at the clarity with which he shared his experience of coming to know the Lord. In brief, his marriage had been in trouble, he had been depressed, in debt, and hooked on pornography as a younger man. One day, his boss took him to lunch and asked him if he had ever received Christ as his Savior. When his boss got a "no" answer, he shared with Byron his own testimony, and told him that we're all sinners, that sin's penalty is death, and that Christ died for our sins and paid our penalty for us. He told him that if he would surrender his life to Jesus Christ, he, too, could have all his sins forgiven and start a new life. It wasn't long; it wasn't elaborate—just person-to-person testimony. Byron told me that right then and there he had decided to become a Christian. I was impressed with

Byron's testimony. I asked him if he had ever shared it with anyone else. He hadn't, but assured me he would.

I've always loved the story of the conversion of the Samaritan woman at the well. The Bible tells us that after she received Christ as her Messiah, she went back into the city and told all she met about what the Lord had done in her life.

> Many of the Samaritans from that town believed in him because of the woman's testimony.
> John 4:39

We don't have the complete text of her testimony. The Bible says she told them that she had met a man who told her all she had ever done. But I believe there was more. I think she must have shared with them how her life had been one large zero before meeting Christ, that now her sins were forgiven, that she had new power to live a victorious life, and that her life now had purpose. The point is, many came to the Lord not by the eloquence of an expert but by the simple testimony of a former prostitute. In the words of the man born blind in John 9, "I was blind but now I see!"

On the back of a box containing a pen I received as a gift, the motto of the company was printed: "Our product speaks for itself." So confident were they about the pen they had created, they could use that slogan. We are God's new creation; and we, the "product," ought to speak for ourselves.

A man in our church who once owned a restaurant never advertised in the local newspaper. When I asked why, he said, "Our best advertisement is satisfied customers. They tell others on their own."

Someone has defined evangelism as "One poor beggar telling another poor beggar where he found the bread."

Good definition! I believe personal testimony is exactly what Peter had in mind when he wrote,

> Always be prepared to give an answer to every-one who asks you to give the reason for the hope that you have.
>
> 1 Peter 3:15

The "answer" is our testimony. When people look at us and realize we are different, we need to be ready to tell them why. I once read that if we don't have a testimony, *we* are a mission field!

There Is an Inherent Power in the Gospel

The Gospel of Jesus Christ includes the death, burial, and resurrection of Jesus Christ. No matter how we share it, its message is powerful enough to break even the most hardened sinner.

> I am not ashamed of the gospel, because it is the *power* of God for the salvation of everyone who believes.
>
> Romans 1:16

I believe there is a connection between this and what Jesus told the apostles in Acts 1:8: "You will receive *power*." At no time do we experience God's power more profoundly than when we're telling people the old, old story. And guess what? Even when we feel we're inept and not telling it exactly right, God still uses it.

This makes me think of a personal experience I had a few years back. I was in the process of training two people in evangelism. We had an appointment to share the gospel with a young couple, but I had an awful headache and was sneezing from allergies. I felt terrible, but we kept the appointment anyway. I was following a simple outline that we teach our trainees to use. In between sneezes and with my head pounding, I tried to stay on track, but I kept losing my concentration. In short, I "butchered" the gospel. Mercifully, I brought our session to a close and asked the couple if they would like to think about what I said and told them we could probably come back next week (something we teach our trainees never to do!). I was shocked to hear the couple say, "Oh no, we would like to become Christians right now, if that's all right." You could have spooned me off the floor. That night, two more souls were added to the kingdom, but *not because I did a great job sharing the Gospel,* but because there is an inherent power in that message—independent of the teller! So, even if you think you're not a good "talker," take courage! Whatever you lack in eloquence, God will make up in his power. That's why Paul wrote,

> My message and my preaching were not with wise and persuasive words, but with a demonstration of the Spirit's power, so that your faith might not rest on men's wisdom, but on God's power.
>
> 1 Corinthians 2:4–5

The gospel had a powerful effect in the pagan city of Corinth, not because an eloquent, charismatic personality came in and wowed them, but because God accompanied the message with his promised power. Take heart; whatever you share of Jesus will be honored!

Every Believer Should Pray for the Unsaved

Is it really biblical to pray for the lost, since the work of salvation is the work of God? Yes. Paul prayed for the lost.

> Brothers, my heart's desire and prayer to God for the Israelites is that they may be saved.
> Romans 10:1

I can't prove it, but I believe Paul prayed daily for his fellow Jews that they would come to know Christ as Savior.

I have a prayer list for the unsaved. Every Wednesday, I pray for people by name who are without Christ. How should we pray for the lost? Everyone has their own way, but I have found the following helpful to me.

First, acknowledge to God that you agree with Scripture that it's his will that they be saved.

> He is patient with you, not wanting anyone to perish, but everyone to come to repentance.
> 2 Peter 3:9

Notice the word "everyone." The gospel is for all. All are invited to the banquet table; all are offered forgiveness. Paul wrote to young Timothy,

> This is good and pleases God our Savior, who
> wants *all* men to be saved and to come to a
> knowledge of the truth.
>
> 1 Timothy 2:3–4

Again, in the Old Testament God himself says,

> Do I take any pleasure in the death of the
> wicked? declares the Sovereign Lord. Rather, am
> I not pleased when they turn from their ways
> and live?
>
> Ezekiel 18:23

When you are witnessing, you are doing something
that God likes, something that's his will, something that
he strongly desires. Since we're to pray for those things
that are according to his will (1 John 5:14), we're always
on safe ground praying for the lost.

Second, ask God to open the eyes of the unsaved so
they can see, because they have been blinded by Satan to
keep them from seeing the light of the Gospel.

> The god of this age has blinded the minds of
> unbelievers, so that they cannot see the light of
> the gospel of the glory of Christ, who is the image
> of God.
>
> 2 Corinthians 4:4

So it's appropriate, I believe, to first command Satan to
let that person go, to tell him that he has no right to his or
her soul and that Jesus died to set that person free. Then
we need to ask God to open our loved one's eyes so they
can see the light of the gospel of Christ.

Finally, pray that God will cross the path of the person
you're praying for with someone who will have a lasting

impact for good on his or her life. God is in the divine appointment business. He, in his providence, has a way of orchestrating people and circumstances to cause the unbeliever to hear and respond to the gospel. It's exciting to pray to that end for our loved ones and friends. That's why we need to look for opportunities to greatly influence others for the sake of the gospel. Who knows, we may be the answer to someone else's prayer.

God Sovereignly Draws People to Salvation

While no once can really "reconcile" the sovereignty of God with the free will of man, one thing is sure: No one can come to Christ unless the Lord draws him. Jesus said,

> No one can come to me unless the Father who sent me draws him.
>
> John 6:44

Jesus repeats this truth later in that same chapter.

> This is why I told you that no one can come to me unless the Father has enabled him.
>
> John 6:65

I believe this is a very important teaching for us to understand. The work of salvation is the work of God, not man. Men and women respond only because they've been "enabled" to do so. We're taught elsewhere in Scripture that before we're saved, in our natural state, we're in a condition of death.

> You were dead in your transgressions and sins.
>
> Ephesians 2:1

When one is dead physically, he is in a state of having no ability to respond to stimuli. When one is dead spiritually, the same is true. We are unresponsive to any outside stimuli, so in order to respond to the Gospel, we must be "made alive."

> Because of his great love for us, God, who is rich in mercy, made us alive with Christ even when we were dead in transgressions.
>
> Ephesians 2:4–5

> When you were dead in your sins and in the uncircumcision of your sinful nature, God made you alive with Christ.
>
> Colossians 2:13

Not only does God provide the salvation, he provides the enablement for us to respond to that salvation. Maybe you've not witnessed to others because you've thought, "What's the use? They're too far gone." While it's true that they are unable to respond in and of themselves because they are spiritually dead, God can "draw" or "enable" them to respond once they've heard the Gospel. The power is in the Gospel of Christ!

God has his own ways of doing the "drawing" or the "enabling." Sometimes it's through a crisis, sometimes it's through a trial, and sometimes it's through the most unsuspecting people and/or circumstances.

God Uses Both the Witness and the Holy Spirit

The work of evangelism is the result of God combining the Holy Spirit and the human witness. Each has a role that God has ordained. The role of the Holy Spirit is clear from Scripture: he is to convince (convict) the sinner of his sin. Jesus said of the Holy Spirit,

> When he comes, he will convict the world of guilt in regard to sin.
>
> John 16:8

His role is unique. He does something we're powerless to do. The work of conviction lies completely out of our purview. We can tell the story, but we cannot do the convicting. That's his work alone. Once the message has fallen on the heart of the unbeliever, the Holy Spirit goes to work. If we try to do his job and be "convincing," we will botch the process.

On the other hand, we have a job to do too: our role is to do the witnessing, the telling. That's our work alone. The Holy Spirit won't do it for us. If we leave to the Spirit what God has ordained for us, we will, again, botch the process.

There are two distinctly different roles for two different people. God combines them to bring about his effectual work of salvation in the sinner's life.

Remember the great promise from God's Word that I shared a couple of chapters ago:

> So is my word that goes out from my mouth: It will not return to me empty, but will accomplish

what I desire, and achieve the purpose for which
I sent it.

Isaiah 55:11

That lets me know that no matter how dismal my witness may "appear" to be, God will see to it that it accomplishes exactly what he purposes. That's a comfort to my
heart. We have been told to tell, we have been won to win,
and we have been saved to serve others the same message
that changed our lives.

More People Come to Christ by the Witness of Friends Than by Any Other Means

Many different surveys have proven this fact. Well
over 90 percent of people who accept Christ do so
through the influence of a friend, relative, or acquain-
tance. The closer the relationship to the person, the
greater the influence. This explodes the idea that people
will come to Christ because we hand them a tract on the
street or preach in a stadium or try to evangelize by television or radio. I'm not saying people don't come to
Christ by those latter means, but far more come to Christ
through personal witness than through any other means.

If it is true that most people are won by the influence
of their friends, it behooves us to develop friendships
with non-Christians. And as we develop and maintain
these friendships, we must take care that our interest in
our new friends is genuine and that we are not just after

their spiritual "scalps." In the words of Paul to the Thessalonians,

> We loved you so much that we were delighted to share with you not only the gospel of God but our lives as well, *because you had become so dear to us.*
> 1 Thessalonians 2:8

Did you catch the tenderness and personal relationship there? "You had become so dear to us." We cannot influence for Christ those we do not deeply care for. It is a cheap evangelism that puts witnessing on the level of depositing an impersonal Gospel into an impersonal person, in an impersonal way. We cannot win those we will not love!

Can you list your non-Christian friends right now? Someone has beautifully said, *Evangelism is mouth-to-ear resuscitation!* How true, how true.

People Are Lost, Doomed, and Damned without Jesus Christ!

This last principle is certainly not the least. Unless we strongly believe this truth, we won't be effective witnesses. The Bible makes it clear that Jesus is God's final and only offer for the remedy of man's sins.

> I am the way and the truth and the life. No one comes to the Father except through me.
> John 14:6

Those words of Jesus say a lot. They say that Christ is God's exclusive way to himself. We either come by him, or we don't come at all! Again, Luke wrote,

> Salvation is found in no one else, for there is no other name under heaven given to men by which we must be saved.
>
> Acts 4:12

You may be saying, "That's a very narrow statement!" Yes, it *is* a narrow statement, but Jesus made it clear in the Sermon on the Mount that the gate is wide and the way is easy that leads to destruction and that many find it; but the gate is *narrow* and the way is hard that leads to life, and few find it. We must come by way of Christ, or we won't come at all.

All of this says that people may be good, kind, lovable, and friendly, but without Jesus Christ, they're as lost as a straight pin in space! No matter how nice or wonderful or unselfish people may be, unless they've been born again, they will not enter the Kingdom of God (John 3:5). This ought to increase our urgency to share with others.

B ut I can hear some of you saying, "Bob, how will witnessing to others help me with my struggle to maintain a victorious walk?" There is only one thing we will do better here on earth than we'll do in heaven—win souls to Jesus Christ! In heaven we'll praise better, we'll love better, we'll get along perfectly with others, and we'll live righteously; but evangelism is the one work we can do better here than in heaven. (After all, there will be no prospects in heaven.) Since those whom we influence for the gospel examine our lives with magnifying glasses, we are motivated to live godly lives—and that helps us maintain our victorious walk!

Do you have a passion for victory? Do you want to walk triumphantly every day? Gossiping the Gospel is one of the best things you can do to ensure that you *stay* on the road of victory. Rememer: If the intake exceeds the output, the upkeep will be the downfall. In other words, if all we do is soak up the truth and never share it, trying to maintain all we've taken in will eventually bring us down.

Well, what about Byron? I wish you could see him at this writing. His middle initial is W for witnessing—he's a witnessing machine! He tells me that while he may slip up from time to time, over the long haul he lives his life with a passion, walking in victory and confidence. In his own words, "When you spend a lot of time talking to others about Christ, you don't have time to do much slipping." I like that philosophy.

Prayer

Lord, I've been won to win, saved to share, and redeemed to repeat. Help me to have holy boldness to share with others what you have done in my life. Enable me to be sensitive to the divine appointments you prepare for me daily.

Amen.

Harnessing Your Trials for Victory

- **Unchanging principles from God's Word**

  Trials produce perseverance

  Trials drive us to dependency on God

  Trials bring a maturity attained no other way

  Our positive reaction to trials can affect others

  We are promised strength equal to the challenge

- **God works all together for good**

- **The choice is yours— sour lemons or lemonade**

- **More than conquerors**

Being Better, Not Bitter

Harnessing Your Trials for Victory

In the days of heavy train travel, a man boarded a train in Baltimore and gave implicit instructions to the porter to awaken him in Columbus, where the train would arrive at 3 A.M. "It is imperative that I get off this train in Columbus. I sometimes get violent when awakened from a deep sleep. I will probably curse you and insist that you let me go back to sleep, but you must not listen to me—no matter what I say. Even if you have to throw me off the train, that is what I want you to do—no matter what!" The next morning the man woke up still on the train. He was furious! He jumped up, found the porter, and gave him a piece of his mind. As he walked away, another porter said, "Boy, was that man ever mad!"

The first porter answered, "If you think he was mad, you should have seen the man I threw off the train in Columbus!"

Some days things just don't go right. The tire goes flat, the car won't start, the furnace breaks, traffic makes you late for work, and on and on it goes. *Trials!* They are a part of life, and no one is exempt. Jesus said that it rains on the just and unjust alike. No one is immune to hardship, trials, and troubles. It's not easy to live triumphantly when dart after dart of discouragement keeps coming at you.

I will never forget Keith and Sue (fictitious names, but real people). They had been believers for about five years when their lives began unraveling. Over a period of six months, a series of events devastated their family. It began when their eight-year-old son was diagnosed with leukemia. Because Keith had recently changed jobs, his hospital insurance was not yet full strength and would only pay one-half benefits. In only three weeks, their medical bills went into the tens of thousands of dollars. Next, Sue was in an automobile accident and was injured fairly seriously. More medical bills. Keith's other car lost its transmission, and soon they were three months behind in their house payments. I learned of Keith's problems when he came by my office to "unload." He showed me a letter from his mortgage company telling him he would lose his house in thirty days unless a payment could be mailed in. Through some friends and a relative, we scraped up enough money for that house payment, but eventually they did lose their house and had to move into a small apartment. Two months later, Keith's company informed him they were downsizing, and he had a choice of taking a substantial cut in pay or being laid off. He took the pay cut, but problems mounted further. Between his wife's exorbitant medical bills and his son's spiraling expenses, Keith became depressed. We read Scripture and prayed. He shared with me how hard it was for him to walk in victory when all around him was one defeat after another. Perhaps more people have trouble maintaining the victorious walk because of trials than anything else.

The lessons Keith and Sue were to learn I will seek to put on paper here.

Unchanging Principles from God's Word

The following principles mined out of God's Word can change your attitude and help you live victoriously even in the most difficult circumstances.

Trials Produce Perseverance

James gives us divine insight:

> Consider it pure joy, my brothers, whenever you face trials of many kinds, because you know that the testing of your faith develops perseverance.
> James 1:2–3

Without going to the University of Trials, we would never learn how to persevere. God's diploma of perseverance only comes as he uses trials to shape our lives. Paul said it this way,

Not only so, but we also rejoice in our sufferings, because we know that suffering produces perseverance; perseverance, character; and character, hope.

Romans 5:3

Trials Drive Us to Dependency On God

As a result of the fall, we all have an independent streak in us that needs to be broken from time to time. Sometimes God allows trials to enter our lives in order to drive us to lean on him and not our human resources. Paul experienced this very thing.

We do not want you to be uninformed, brothers, about the hardships we suffered in the province of Asia. We were under great pressure, far beyond our ability to endure, so that we despaired even of life. Indeed, in our hearts we felt the sentence of death. But this happened that we might not rely on ourselves but on God.

2 Corinthians 1:8–9

The old adage "It wasn't till I was on my back that I looked up to God" is more true than we might think. From time to time, all of us need to be reminded that apart from the Lord, we really can do nothing.

Trials Bring a Maturity Attained No Other Way

In his little epistle about trials James goes on to say,

Perseverance must finish its work so that you may be mature and complete, not lacking in anything.

James 1:4

Just as metal becomes stronger after going through the crucible of fire, so we emerge from the fire of trials with a greater strength, perspective, and maturity. The giant oak trees on the Gulf Coast are so hard that a saw will barely cut through them. Why? Because they are subject to the violent winds coming off the gulf in the spring and summer. The wind has a way of twisting and bending those trees. Over the years, that makes them tougher than trees not affected by wind. The harder the storms, the tougher the trees! The same is true in life. People who haven't been shielded from the storms of life are stronger, more mature, and more sensitive to others.

Our Positive Reaction to Trials Can Affect Others

God can bring blessings from even the most difficult trials that come into our lives. One blessing he brings is that our positive reaction to these trials can be used as an object lesson for someone needing a great witness. I recall an incident back in the '70s, when a little five-year-old boy in our church was hospitalized with cancer. For over six weeks, he and his godly parents bravely fought off the angels of death that knocked at his door daily. He finally went home to be with the Lord. In watching his parents' reaction to this tragedy, one doctor and two head nurses gave their hearts to the Lord. In her testimony, one of the nurses said, "If Christ can enable someone to go through that without becoming bitter, then I want him in my life as well."

Our trials can also be used as stepping stones to bless others. Who can better identify with a woman who's had a miscarriage than another woman who's had a miscarriage? Who can come alongside someone who's lost a loved one to cancer better than someone who's gone through the same ordeal? Who can have an impact on a drug or alcohol addict like one who has himself been delivered from an addiction?

I'm thinking of a dear man in our church who, after thirty-two years with a company, became the victim of downsizing. He went to work one day to discover that he no longer had a job. It's not easy to get another job at fifty-two years old. His whole life changed, as did his standard of living. He was eventually forced to take a job paying less than half his previous salary. Humiliated, discouraged, and depressed, he determined to use this experience to help other men going through the same thing. He began a prayer and encouragement group for such men, and what once had seemed disastrous God turned into a blessing for himself and many other men.

We Are Promised Strength Equal to the Challenge

While we aren't promised exemption from struggles and trails, we are promised strength to get us through them. Listen to some of these promises:

> Cast your cares on the Lord and he will sustain you; he will never let the righteous fall.
> Psalm 55:22

God is our refuge and strength, an ever-present help in trouble.

Psalm 46:1

When you pass through the waters, I will be with you; and when you pass through the rivers, they will not sweep over you. When you walk through the fire, you will not be burned; the flames will not set you ablaze.

Isaiah 43:2

Over and over again in God's Word, we are promised direction, strength, help, and comfort for the times when we're going through the thick of it. Nowhere in Scripture are we promised immunity from trials. Both Christians and non-Christians will have some dark days. What we do with them and how we handle them is colored by our relationship to God in Jesus Christ.

I suppose nothing illustrates this point better than the story of the man walking down the beach under a heavy burden. For a long while, God walked beside the man, leaving two sets of footprints in the sand. Soon there was only one set of footprints in the sand. The burdened man complained, "Lord, where did you go? Where were you when I needed you most?" God responded, "You see only one set of prints in the sand because when your burden became too heavy for you to bear, I picked you up and carried you." In your darkest hour, God is not only with you, he picks you up and carries you when all your strength is gone.

A Christian state patrolman in our church stopped a car for excessive speeding on the freeway. The young unmarried couple inside were on their way to get an abortion. That patrolman offered solace to the upset woman by asking her if she wanted or needed any further counsel. Her response was a quick "yes." He offered to escort them to our church ministry that helps unwed mothers make right decisions. He was later charged with obstructing an abortion and using his position as a law-enforcement officer to impose his convictions on someone else, and he eventually lost his job. His name was drug through the mud in the press, and his young family was humiliated by many false accusations. But through it all, he found his strength in the Lord, even during the darkest days before and during his trial. After more than a year and a half of wrangling, he finally lost his job. Even then, he was able to say, "Praise God for what he's allowing me to go through, because I know he is still with me." It's comforting to know that even when injustice prevails, the Lord has not abandoned you.

God Works All Together for Good

I'm convinced that everything that happens to me in this life is either God caused or God allowed. In either case, God is sovereignly in total control. If my trial was "sent" to me by God for discipline or preparation, I need to trust his wise decision. If my trial was "allowed" by him to teach me valuable lessons for the future, he needs my full compliance. Paul said it like this,

> And we know that in all things God works for the good of those who love him, who have been called according to his purpose.
>
> Romans 8:28

How true that affirmation is! That Scripture reminds me of my grandmother. Years ago when I'd go to visit her, her back porch, which doubled as her sewing room, would be stacked high with hundreds of strands of cloth—all shapes, colors, and sizes. They made no sense to me, and I could have easily called them rags. But I'd go back six months later and see on her bed a multi-colored quilt with a beautiful pattern reflecting symmetry and creativity. All I saw the first time was unconnected pieces. Through the process of quilting, they were all brought together for a beautifully designed quilt.

Isn't that the way life is? All we see is the here and now—cancer, death, loss, tragedy—it doesn't make any sense to us. What we forget is that it's part of the whole garment God is weaving for our lives. No wonder David could say,

> The boundary lines have fallen for me in pleasant places; surely I have a delightful inheritance.
> Psalm 16:6

I love that passage. David was advanced in years and was looking back over his whole life. David's life had been filled with tragedy as well as triumph: he had been hunted and hounded by King Saul, he had suffered severe depression following his sin with Bathsheba and his murder of her husband, and he had walked through many dark nights of the soul. But in reflecting on his life, he realized that the dark threads were as needful as the bright-colored ones. God is weaving our lives together as well.

Some of you, as you are reading these very words, may be going through illness . . . financial collapse . . . marital disaster . . . family tragedy . . . deep grief . . . depression. If with myopic vision, you see only that event, it will do you in; but if you see it as a necessary chapter in the book God is writing about your life, you'll walk in victory and joy.

The Choice Is Yours— Sour Lemons or Lemonade

Many years ago in another city, I was in the habit of visiting in the nursing homes every other week. Usually, they were depressing places, filled with cynical, complaining, hurting people. But there was one resident I looked forward to seeing. Her name was Ernestine. In her 80s, she sat daily in her wheelchair, drawn up almost beyond recognition with rheumatoid arthritis. She had had it from childhood and had been confined to a wheelchair at twenty-one, when she could no longer walk. No husband, no children or grandchildren—she missed all of that because of her disease. Her little limbs had become so stiff and gnarled that she could no longer feed or tend to herself. Her head was bent down to her chest, and she used a mirror to see her visitors, which were very few. But what she lacked in physical attractiveness, she made up for in effervescent joy! She was a delight to be around, and I always left cheered up. When I knew I was moving away and would never see her again in this life, I said to her, "Ernestine, I have to ask you something: Having sat for over sixty years in that chair, deprived of family, fun, and the ability to walk, how can you be so cheerful?" I'll never forget her answer.

"Well, Preacher, it's like this—when life throws you a lemon, you can do one of two things: you can suck it and be sour, or you can squeeze it and make lemonade. I chose the latter, and my life has been good!"

I could hardly believe my ears! "My life has been good." But I've never forgotten her analogy. Lemonade! That's the secret.

I've known many Christians in the past who stayed on top and basked in victory until . . . the trials came. Then they allowed the exigencies of life to prevent them from walking victoriously. In essence, they chose to suck the lemon and be sour rather than to make lemonade. What about you?

More Than Conquerors

> But we have this treasure in jars of clay to show that this all-surpassing power is from God and not from us. We are hard pressed on every side, but not crushed; perplexed, but not in despair; persecuted, but not abandoned; struck down, but not destroyed.
>
> 2 Corinthians 4:7–9

Paul was insulted, cursed, discriminated against, put down, and almost killed, and he lived at the mercy of the provision of his friends. In all this, he still said,

> We are more than conquerors through him who loved us.
>
> Romans 8:37

How could he possibly say "We are more than conquerors" after all he'd been through? How can we claim victory when we are beset by trials? I think there are two ways.

First, you are a conqueror because in Christ, and only
in Christ, you are a "somebody." Years and years ago,
there was a popular tune whose main lyrics were "You're
nobody till somebody loves you." In a sense, we're
nobody until we experience the redeeming love of God, at
which point we become children of God. Our life of
defeat before we knew Christ is so far removed from our
victorious life in Christ that the two cannot even be com-
pared. Just being in Christ makes us conquerors.

But there is another sense in which we are more than
conquerors. As Christians, we have access to God's
power, God's direction, and God's inexhaustible supply
of wisdom. That makes us super conquerors. We have
access to what non-Christians don't have access to—
namely, the riches of our God. That means that nothing
can do us in, unless we just allow it.

I cannot but think of the words of Job. After all he
lost—his health, his money, his children, his wife's
respect, his friends' empathy—he was still able to say,

> I know that my Redeemer lives, and that in the
> end he will stand upon the earth.
>
> Job 19:25

How could he say that? How could he have such optimism in the midst of such overwhelming loss? Because,
as he later said,

> He knows the way that I take; when he has tested
> me, I will come forth as gold.
>
> Job 23:10

You see, Job knew something you and I tend to forget. These struggles and trials through which we're compelled to go are designed by God to refine us, to sharpen us, to make us pure and free from all alloy.

I'm amazed at the ultimate outcome of Job's life. The Bible says that the Lord made him prosperous again and gave him twice as much as he had before (Job 42:10). Job went through some deep and dark valleys, but in the end, God put him back on top. I believe that through it all, Job remained victorious and refused to let his hardships harden him against God. We need to do the same.

So, if you're going through a furnace of trials right now, take heart! It's either God allowed or God caused. Either way, God is sovereignly in charge, and he has promised to go with you through that trial and bring you out at the other end *better*, not *bitter*, if you'll only cooperate. It's easy (it's our nature) to whine, complain, and have a pity party over our trials—but that will make us *bitter*. The other option is to give thanks in everything and believe that God is up to something good in our lives—and that's *better*.

You can be bitter or better—the choice is yours. If you decide to be better, your passion for victory will keep you in the victor's circle.

Oh, yes, remember Keith and Sue? You'll be glad to know that their son's leukemia is in full remission, Sue recuperated from her injuries, Keith landed a job paying more than his original one, and they "dug out" of what appeared to be a hopeless situation. I don't think they could have done it without learning the unchanging principles from God's Word that I shared in this chapter.

Though they were tempted, they never let go of the promises of God and were thus able to maintain their triumphant walk with him. Today they are more secure in their victory for having gone through and graduated from the University of Trials.

Keith and Sue had a choice: they could become *bitter* or *better!* They chose to become better by the grace of God. How about you?

Prayer

Lord, thank you for the trials that are nipping at my heels right now. Give me the grace not to avoid them but to learn from them. Save me from a bitter spirit and a resentful attitude. Help me trust where I cannot see and hope where all seems doubtful. When I'm ready to throw in the towel, remind me of Gethsemane and the time when all your disciples forsook you and fled and the cross loomed large over your head. Show me how to count it all joy when those trials come my way.

Amen.

Getting You to the Finish Line

- Rejoice in God's unconditional love
- Resist Satan's plan
- Resign from the world system
- Remember: your remake is a process
- Rely on the Lord
- Resolve to be victorious

Tips for the Trip

Getting You to the Finish Line

S everal years ago, when I was planning to take my family across the country on a two-week vacation, I ordered and received a trip packet from a national auto club. The kit contained not only a map of how to get from where we lived to where we were going, but a helpful little booklet titled "Tips for the Trip." It was essentially a "survival" booklet for families traveling long distances in a car. It gave pertinent information on roadside parks, campgrounds, highway conditions, eating places, and games you could play to make the time go more quickly. Very helpful!

The Christian life is a "trip." We begin at the "on-ramp" of conversion, and we don't get off till we're "home." But what happens between point A and point Z is largely up to us—under the hand of a sovereign God, of course. We can make the trip with joy and victory, or we can make the trip in defeat and agony. The choice is ours.

This book has been about living in victory instead of spiking up and down—one day on top, the next day on bottom. It's been about the formula for success in our Christian walk. For too many, the Christian life is like a roller-coaster ride: for a few days they fly high in victory and the power of the Holy Spirit, then for a week or two they nosedive into carnality, defeat, and failure. It's a yo-yo existence that brings frustration, disappointment, and, yes, even anger.

When Lew cornered me one evening after a Bible conference session, his appraisal of his past fifty years was a sad one. Now sixty-nine years old, he acknowledged that all of his fifty-five years as a Christian had been, for the most part, a disappointment. In his words, "An elevator doesn't go up and down in a day as many times as I do spiritually." His moments of victory were too few and too seldom. Oh, he knew he would go to heaven when he died; he had assurance of his eternal salvation since it was based on the finished work of Christ. But the heaven he was supposed to have experienced on earth had eluded him. We talked for almost an hour, and I shared with him some of the following tips for the trip that I think are all-important.

Rejoice in God's Unconditional Love

It's so easy for us to forget that God loves us unconditionally—whether we are in victory or defeat. Our performance doesn't change his love for us. Some feel that their behavior affects God's ability to love them. But victory cannot increase God's love, and our defeats don't diminish it.

No, being confident of God's love isn't a license to live in defeat or be carnal; it's a reminder that we are loved by him and that his love isn't based on our performance or our worthiness. Paul said,

> God has poured out his love into our hearts by the Holy Spirit whom he has given us.
> Romans 5:5

John, in his first epistle, defined real love by reminding us that God took the *initiative* in loving us.

> This is love: not that we loved God, but that he loved us and sent his Son as an atoning sacrifice for our sins.
> 1 John 4:10

And God doesn't just release his love eye-dropper style—one little drop at a time:

> How great is the love the Father has *lavished* on us, that we should be called children of God!
> 1 John 3:1

John said God "lavishes" his love on us. We have a little more motivation to translate our passion for victory into action if we know we're loved even if we fall. Falling down doesn't mean we have fallen out of our salvation nor does it mean we have drifted beyond the scope of his love. We may be temporarily "struck down," as Paul said in 2 Corinthians 4, but we can never be pushed out of his circle of love. His is the love that "will not let us go." It's the love that lifts, lasts, and covers our most despicable behavior. Your "trip" through this life with Christ will be much more joyous if you know that God won't pull back on his love for you. This doesn't mean that he condones all we do nor does it mean he simply chooses to look the other way, but it does mean that nothing we do or fail to do can change his love for us. What a comfort.

Resist Satan's Plan

Since the devil failed in his plan to stop you from becoming a Christian, he has resorted to plan B. Now his tactics are aimed at making you a *miserable* Christian, and the best way he can do that is by keeping you in defeat. But you must resist him: he has no authority except what you grant him. So don't give an inch! But remember, he's a persistent devil, so be on guard. Even when tempting the Son of God, he tried three times to get Jesus to cave in and serve him. All three times, with Scripture, Jesus rebuked him and put him in his place. We need to do the same. I like this promise from James,

> Resist the devil, and he will flee from you.
> James 4:7

Peter, in his first epistle, reminds us that the devil is like a roaring lion seeking someone to devour, then he bids us,

> Resist him, standing firm in the faith.
> 1 Peter 5:9

As I mentioned in a previous chapter, we need to get serious and verbal with the devil and not request, but demand, that he get off our premises. He comes to steal, kill, and destroy. First, he tries to steal our assurance; then he attempts to kill our fight; and finally, he tries to destroy our testimony and our positive influence on others. He will do all of that if we permit him. It's up to us to resist him.

Resign from the World System

Wait a minute! Lest you think I'm suggesting a radical asceticism or a hermit existence, hear me out!

Mere separation from the world and outward observance of rules and regulations certainly won't insure victory. Right after I became a Christian, I attended a tent meeting conducted by what we called "Holy Rollers." They were a rare combination of Pentecostal, Wesleyan, and Armenian people who went to an extreme in their outward show of holiness. They were not allowed to play cards, go to movies, smoke, drink, dance, or play games. The women were not permitted to cut their hair or wear any kind of makeup, jewelry, short-sleeved blouses, or swimsuits. They were separatists. For the most part, non-holiness people, I remember, laughed at them, ignored them, or heckled them. They were seen, even by other religious groups, as aberrant and most definitely overboard.

In retrospect, however, while they may have dwelt too much on outward holiness, they at least drew a line in the sand and had enough respect for the holiness of God to take holy living seriously. Today, I would choose their extreme lifestyle over the indulgent, loose, compromising lifestyle of many Christians, who go to the other extreme and play footsie with the world in order to prove their freedom in Christ.

If we're going to be successful on this trip of life, we need to decide up front what our relationship with the world and its system will be. Yes, we must live in the world; and true, it's not easy living in a place without reflecting that place. Yet Scripture is clear:

> Do not love the world or anything in the world. If anyone loves the world, the love of the Father is not in him.
>
> 1 John 2:15

James gets even more specific:

> Don't you know that friendship with the world is hatred toward God? Anyone who chooses to be a friend of the world becomes an enemy of God.
>
> James 4:4

Strong words! If you truly have a passion for victory, you must resign from (with no thought of going back) the world—its value system, its philosophy, its song, its direction. While we must live in the world, we must not conform to its values.

Maybe this is why Paul adamantly said in Colossians,

> Since, then, you have been raised with Christ, set your hearts on things above, where Christ is seated at the right hand of God. Set your minds on things above, not on earthly things.
>
> Colossians 3:1–2

Get your focus off of this fleeting, passing world system, and place it on Christ. This means refusal to fall into the trap of the world's monetary system, its mores, its code of ethics, and its idea of worth.

We weren't meant to grovel in the dirt on the level of the world. We, who were made to have a personal relationship with the Almighty God, were never meant to settle down in this common and mundane world, any more than the wild eagle was meant to come down and be content to scratch the dirt for food in the chicken coop. Someone has said that it seems incredible that we who were made for a heavenly existence should accept this world as our ultimate home.

We cannot live in triumph and live by the rules of the world system at the same time. We're in the world, but not of it. And as long as we are in this world, we will live in constant tension—torn between our heavenly citizenship and our earthly responsibilities. True, our jobs are in this world system, most schools are in this world system, and we shop in this world system; but we don't have to dance to its music.

> Our citizenship is in heaven.
> Philippians 3:20

Remember:
Your Remake Is a Process

That's right. I said "remake," because that's the process that God is taking us all through.

> And we, who with unveiled faces all reflect the
> Lord's glory, are being *transformed into his likeness*
> with ever-increasing glory, which comes from the
> Lord, who is the Spirit.
>
>   2 Corinthians 3:18

Isn't that amazing? God is shaping us into the likeness
of Jesus Christ! But it's a process, mind you, not a completed job. In one sense, we are God's "projects."

Years ago, I often saw bumper stickers that said "P B P
W M G I N F W M Y." It stood for "Please be patient with
me, God is not finished with me yet." If we want to live
triumphantly every day, we must remember that we are
in flux; we are being changed into his glory, day by day,
piece by piece, little by little. The trip will be much more
meaningful if we remember that we are in process.

As a kid, I would sometimes fall out of bed. It was a
scary experience. My father would come and pick me up
and put me back in bed, and he'd say, "Son, everyone falls
out of bed once in awhile. It's no shame to fall out; it's a
shame to *stay* out!" He was right. Remember, your
remake is an ongoing change.

Rely on the Lord

I'm not talking about relying on the Lord to help you
gain the victory by your *own* efforts; I'm talking about
relying on the Lord to live *his* life *through* you, thus bring-
ing you to victory. I cannot, by my own wit, strength, and
cleverness live victoriously every day. I will only maintain victory to the degree that I allow Christ to live his life

in and through me. Jesus said in John 15, "Apart from me, you can do nothing."

There's a dangerous mind-set that invades us all: it's the mind-set that says, "I'm invincible. I can do anything; I can accomplish anything—if I just put my mind to it." This kind of thinking is humanism, *par excellence.* It's like writing out my own agenda and plans and then saying, "Lord, bless my plans." What God really wants us to do is to give him a blank sheet of paper, sign our name at the bottom, and say, "Lord, you fill it in."

When I graduated from high school, I took a job with the government as a clerk typist. I was one of about two hundred in a very large room. The information we were to type was often very difficult and demanded much discernment even before we struck a key. My supervisor was a very sharp young man who knew all the forms by heart. Many times in the midst of a heavy workload and complicated forms that called for accurate judgment, I would wish my supervisor could crawl inside me and do those forms *through* me! That's what Christ desires to do in us!

The Christian life is not a snap. It's very difficult at times. Instead of asking God to "help us get through," we must realize that we can't get through. Only as he lives *in* and *through* us can we make it. Although I've already shared this Ian Thomas quote in an earlier chapter, it bears repeating here: "I can't, Lord, but you never said I could; you can, and you always said you would!"

When I was teaching my son to drive, although his hands were on the steering wheel, my hands were on his hands! I wanted him to get the feel of the wheel, while at the same time protecting both of us. Christ wants to put his hand on ours, too, but we must give him permission to live the Christian life in and through us.

There's one more thing needed to stay in victory.

Resolve to Be Victorious

While I believe we are never defeated as far as our position in Christ is concerned and that our salvation is secure since it's provided by Jesus Christ (he said that "no one will snatch you out of my hand"), I also believe that we can live in varying degrees of victory. While God has made every provision for us to remain victorious in our walk and experience, we must pursue that victory with *resolve.*

I remember lunching with a man who poured out to me the last ten years of his life. His account was terrible and depressing. He told of failure after failure, disappointment after disappointment, carnal living, temptations yielded to, and victories missed. Although he believed he was in Christ, he described his life as a "diet of failure." After a time of conversation, I finally asked him, "Have you seriously *resolved* to live victoriously?" He admitted that he hadn't.

Now, I'm not advocating the heretical teaching that what we confess, we have. I think that is unbiblical. But I am suggesting that we generally do what we resolve to do. Call it a vow, call it a promise, or just a strong resolution, but I've found in my own life that what I *resolve* to do, I usually do! Last summer, I resolved to paint my deck on a particular Saturday. At least three major distractions pulled me away from that project, but guess what? I painted my deck that Saturday! Yes, I realize that just intending to do something won't make it come about, but I'm talking about more than just good intentions. I'm talking about the conviction to back those intentions up.

One of the lines from Robert Robinson's hymn, "Come, Thou Fount of Every Blessing," accurately describes you and me: "Prone to wander, Lord, I feel it, prone to leave the God I love." We *are* prone to wander. We have a great propensity for straying; and without *resolution*, we probably will wander aimlessly. We allow too many distractions to steal our victory. When Jesus "set his face to go to Jerusalem" nothing could have held him back—he was *resolved*. When Paul "determined" to go to Spain, he was truly resolved in his spirit to go. When he wanted to make it clear that his old life and old failures were left behind, he resolutely said so.

> Forgetting what is behind and straining toward what is ahead, I *press on* toward the goal.
>
> Philippians 3:13–14

You can't help but hear a resolute spirit in those words.

Job was a man with a resolute spirit.

> I made a covenant with my eyes not to look lustfully at a girl.
>
> Job 31:1

That meant he was serious. I believe half of remaining in victory is found in *resolving* to stay there.

Not long ago, I penned a prayer to God that depicts my resignation to myself and my resolution to be totally at God's disposal. I hope you make it your prayer too!

Prayer

Lord, I'm clay, made soft by the miracle of your touch. Shape me into whatever you choose—whenever, however, for as long-ever, and for whomever! I'm open to the shape you will make of me.

If you fashion me into a wedge, I'll gladly hold the door open so your gospel can go into all the world; if you press me into a wheel, I'll roll to your destination; if you mold me into a cup, I'll be filled with water for one of your disciples; if you make me into an altar, I'll gladly be knelt upon by any you choose; if you shape me into a scroll, write on me what you will for any to read; if you rub me into a baton, use me to conduct your symphony; if you bend me into a flask, I'll contain your sweet perfume; if you block me into a vase, I'll display the flowers you arrange; if you spin me into a plate, I'll willingly hold food for others; if you pinch me into an arrow, I'll quickly speed to your target; if you create of me a bush, I'll burn for whatever prophet you choose to watch; if you make me into a tree, I'll shade your weary pilgrims; if you twist me into a trumpet, I'll gladly be blown for your praise and glory; if you turn me into a pair of shoes, I'll protect the feet of those who share the gospel of peace; if you fashion me into a plaque, I'll hang joyously on any wall to display your handiwork.

Lord, you're the potter; I'm the clay. Keep me soft, moldable, ready to be shaped into whatever you desire. And, Lord, when the molding is done and my clay is hard, I'll not seek to be something other than what you've made me. Teach me anew that whatever *you make of me is an original!*

Amen.